COPYCAT RECIPES:

Cookbook on How to Make Cracker Barrel Restaurant's Popular Recipes at Home.

Over 80 Recipes

JOE COOK

© Copyright 2020. All rights reserved.

The content contained within this book may not be reproduced, duplicated or transmitted without direct written permission from the author or the publisher.

This book is copyright protected. This book is only for personal use. You cannot amend, use, quote or paraphrase any part, or the content within this book, without the consent of author or publisher.

TABLE OF CONTENTS

INTRODUCTION 4

CHAPTER 1   BREAKFAST 7

1. FRENCH TOAST 7
2. HASH BROWN CASSEROLE 9
3. LOADED HASH BROWN CASSEROLE 10
4. BUTTERMILK PANCAKES 11
5. HAM AND EGG CASSEROLE 12
6. SAWMILL GRAVY AND BISCUITS 13
7. BLUEBERRY SYRUP 14
8. EGGS-IN-THE-BASKET 15
9. AVOCADO EGGROLLS 16
10. HARVEST GRAIN 'N NUT" PANCAKES 18
11. CINNAMON APPLES 19
12. CHEESE 'N' GRITS CASSEROLE 20
13. DELUXE MASHED POTATOES 21
14. SAUSAGE EGG MUFFIN 22

CHAPTER 2   SIDES AND SALADS   23

15. COLESLAW 23
16. GREEN BEANS 25
17. BRUSSELS SPROUT N' KALE SALAD 26
18. CHICKEN POT STICKERS 27
19. LETTUCE WRAPS 28
20. SHRIMP DUMPLINGS 29
21. DRY GARLIC RIBS 30
22. STUFFED MUSHROOMS 31
23. SPINACH ARTICHOKE DIP 32
24. CLAMS BRUSCHETTA 33
25. FRIED MOZZARELLA 34

26. HOT N' SPICY BUFFALO WINGS 35
27. GUACAMOLE 36
28. LOADED POTATO SKINS 37

CHAPTER 3   POULTRY AND FISH 38

29. GRILLED CHICKEN TENDERLOINS 38
30. SUNDAY FRIED CHICKEN 40
31. BROCCOLI CHEDDAR CHICKEN 41
32. OLD COUNTRY STORE DUMPLINGS 42
33. CHICKEN AND DUMPLINGS 44
34. CHICKEN CASSEROLE 46
35. CHICKEN-FRIED STEAK & GRAVY 48
36. SPICY OVEN-FRIED CHICKEN 49
37. SKILLET-GRILLED CATFISH 50
38. COUNTRY CHICKEN WITH GRAVY 51
39. APPLE CIDER BBQ CHICKEN BREAST 52
40. GREEN CHILI JACK CHICKEN 53
41. ORANGE CHICKEN 54
42. FISH TACOS 56

CHAPTER 4   DESSERTS 57

43. FRIED APPLES RECIPE 57
44. OLD COUNTRY STORE DOUBLE FUDGE COCA COLA CAKE 59
45. CHOCOLATE CHIP PECAN PIE 60
46. CHOCOLATE CHERRY COBBLER 61
47. APPLE DUMPLING BAKE 62
48. HOMEMADE CORN MUFFINS WITH HONEY BUTTER 63

49. Peach Cobbler with Almond Crumble Topping 64
50. Banana Pudding 66
51. Campfire S'more 68
52. Strawberry Shortcake 70
53. Pumpkin Custard N' Ginger Snaps 71
54. Old Country Store Carrot Cake 73
55. Cinnabon Cinnamon Swirl Cheesecake 75
56. Peanut Butter Cheesecake 77

CHAPTER 5   BEEF AND PORK 80

57. Beef Stew 80
58. Meat Loaf 82
59. Roast Beef 83
60. Grilled Pork Chops 84
61. Peppered Ribeye Steaks 85
62. Mushroom Braised Pot Roast 86
63. Shepherd's Pie 87
64. Steak Diane 88
65. Pasta Carbonara 89

66. Grilled Steak Medallions 90
67. Provolone Stuffed Meatballs ... 91
68. Brunch Burger 93
69. Quesadilla Burger 94
70. Honey Barbecue Riblets 96

CHAPTER 6   BREAD AND SOUP 98

71. Biscuits and Sausage Gravy 98
72. Buttermilk Biscuits 100
73. Breadsticks 101
74. Chicken Gnocchi Soup 102
75. Zuppa Toscana 103
76. Pasta e Fagioli 104
77. Lima Beans 106
78. Toasted Ravioli 107
79. Chicken Potpie 108
80. Roast Beef Sandwiches with Mashed Potatoes 109
81. Corn Chowder 110
82. Squash Soup 111
83. Cuban Sandwich 112
84. Chicken Noodle Soup 113

CONCLUSION 114

Introduction

The Cracker Barrel is a definite favorite dining choice for many people who are lucky enough to have one nearby. However, some people are not so fortunate. Here you will find some of the Cracker Barrel's most popular and well-loved dishes. You will find here the best and savory dessert and meat recipes that you can make from the comfort of your home

These copycat recipes put the Cracker Barrel menu right at your fingertips. From the iconic French toast to beef stew, any of your Cracker Barrel cravings can be fulfilled at home with this cookbook.

Meals at the restaurant are the greatest. This is why we are pleased that food bloggers and other great chefs recreated a number of meals from our favorite chains (guilty fast food, and so on) there. You may thank these geniuses for enabling you to whip up anything you want and eat while you were lazy on your own couch.

Copycat recipes really please the home cook! Famous copycat recipe is the recipe that you can replicate and cook in your own home from your favorite restaurants. You can now bring the kitchen of your favorite restaurant to your own home with the help of the famous copycat recipe and be the chef to cook hundreds of your favorite gourmet recipes. Cooking at home can take a long time and create chaos that you need to clear up, but once you've finished and tried a particular dish, you're going to be shocked and proud that you've created a very popular, delicious dish and become a professional chef. Surprise you every day, because everything is in your hands with the famous copy of Cracker Barrel's copycat recipe.

Cooking helps together families and home cooking is a great way for your family to get together over the dining table. Everyone enjoys a home-cooked meal— particularly moody teens and chicken eaters. Moreover, if you stay home, that is not preparing, or dining. Sharing meals with others is a great way to broaden the social network. Getting thankful feedback on a meal that you prepared for someone may also give your self-esteem a real boost.

Famous copycat recipes are the recipes in your favorite restaurants at home that you can mimic and prepare. What is the famous imitator recipe? In a restaurant, the chefs usually eat to figure out what ingredients make the food so delicious. The ingredients used the exact measure and the length of time needed for cooking. These have been translated into a new variety and published as a book for the recipe.

Eating is one of the pleasures of life and, when possible, we love to consume the foods we like, and avoid ones we do not prefer. Eating at home is a reason for better health and fitness, experts say. Those who prepare their meals at home tend to eat better and stay in better shape than those who go out. Including more homemade food in your daily life and reducing dependence on packaged food and restaurant costs is beneficial for your well-being for several reasons. The more you cook, the healthier your life. You do not need to be a celebrity chef to transform your usual cooking skills.

You can now add the kitchen of your favorite restaurant to your home with the aid of the popular copycat recipe and, as a chef, prepare hundreds of your favorite gourmet recipes. Say goodbye to a restaurant's long waiting to take a seat, and in particular say goodbye to paying too much every time you visit an expensive restaurant.

Consider your meals a shared activity. The simple act of talking to a friend or a lover at the table will play an important role in alleviating tension and improving mood. Gather the kids together and keep up with each other's everyday life. Invite a relative, partner or neighbor if you stay alone.

It is great to make copycat recipes at home. They give you the exact ingredients, but as you see fit, you can modify them. Whether you want to taste different food or add your own vegetables, it does not matter. You can also add low-fat ingredients or remove allergic ingredients. There are endless possibilities. You are in complete control. Like the original dishes, how do you learn these recipes taste?

These copycat recipes will let you get the taste of these dishes in the comfort of your own home. Just change the relevant ingredients so that the meal will delight you and your family. This cookbook is filled with copycat recipes from Cracker Barrel that you can make at home, some as quickly as 30 minutes. These recipes range from breakfast meals and snacks to entrees and desserts. You will start cooking like a restaurant chef in no time!

In this cookbook, you will find our favorite and classic Cracker Barrel recipes to make at home. So let us get started and prepare a feast our friends and family will remember.

Chapter 1 Breakfast

1. French Toast

Preparation Time: 5 minutes

Cooking Time: 4 to 6 minutes

Servings: 2 to 4

Ingredients:

8 slices Texas toast or sourdough bread 4 eggs 1 cup milk

2 tablespoons sugar

4 teaspoons vanilla extract

2 pinches salt

Butter and syrup for serving

Directions:

Whisk the eggs, milk, sugar, vanilla, and salt together in a large bowl.

Heat a griddle or skillet over medium heat. Spray with nonstick cooking spray.

Dip each slice of bread in egg mixture, letting it soak for 25–30 seconds on each side.

Transfer the slices to the griddle or skillet and cook for 2–3 minutes on each side, or until golden brown.

Serve with butter and syrup.

Nutrition:

Calories: 252,

Carbohydrates: 33g,

Protein: 11g,

Fat: 7g,

Saturated Fat: 2g,

Cholesterol: 167mg,

Sodium: 471mg,

Potassium: 171mg,

Fiber: 1g, Sugar: 8g, Calcium: 201mg, Iron: 2.7mg

2. Hash Brown Casserole

Preparation Time: 10 minutes

Cooking Time: 55 minutes

Servings: 4 to 6

Ingredients: 1 (30-ounce) bag frozen hash browns, thawed ½ cup butter, melted

1 can cream of chicken soup 1 small onion, chopped

1-pound cheddar cheese, shredded (divided) 1 teaspoon salt

½ teaspoon black pepper 1 cup sour cream

Directions:

Preheat oven to 350°F. Prepare a baking dish either by greasing the sides or spraying with nonstick cooking spray.

Mix together the onion, cream of chicken soup, pepper, and all but 1 cup of the shredded cheese in a large bowl. When combined, mix in the sour cream until it is well incorporated.

Add the melted butter and hash browns. Stir to combine. Pour into the greased baking dish.

Bake for 45 minutes or until bubbly, then sprinkle the remaining cheese on top and bake an additional 5–10 minutes or until the cheese is melted.

Nutrition:

Calories: 90 Total Fat: 3.5g Saturated Fat: 2g Trans Fat: 0g Cholesterol: 10mg

Sodium: 160mg Total Carbohydrates: 11g Dietary Fibers: 1g Sugars: 2g Protein: 4g

3. Loaded Hash Brown Casserole

Preparation Time: 15 minutes

Cooking Time: 45 minutes

Servings: 6 to 8

Ingredients: 1-pound sausage 3 tablespoons chopped red bell pepper

½ cup grated American cheese ½ cup grated sharp cheddar cheese

½ cup grated Monterey Jack cheese 1½ cups grated Colby cheese (divided)

2 tablespoons butter 2 tablespoons flour 2 cups milk 2 pounds frozen hash browns

Directions:

Preheat the oven to 350°F. Cook the sausage in a large skillet over medium high heat while breaking it into bite-sized pieces. Add the red pepper and cook. Drain any grease and set to the side. Melt 2 tablespoons of butter in another skillet. Stir in the flour and let it cook for a minute or so until it starts to brown. Whisk in ¼ cup of the milk and continue to cook and stir until the mixture thickens. Then whisk in the remaining milk and cook a bit longer. It will thicken up again; when it does, add the cheeses, reserving 1 cup of the Colby cheese for the top of the casserole. In a bowl, combine the hash browns, the cheese sauce you just prepared, and the cooked sausage. Mix together so that everything is combined, then pour into a baking dish and top with the reserved Colby cheese. Cook for about 45 minutes or until the cheese is melted and the casserole is bubbly.

Nutrition: Calories: 520, Carbohydrates: 25g, Protein: 24g, Fat: 35g, Saturated

Fat: 17g, Cholesterol: 100mg, Sodium: 814mg, Potassium: 607mg, Fiber: 1g,

Sugar: 3g, Calcium: 450mg, Iron: 2.2mg

4. Buttermilk Pancakes

Preparation Time: 5 minutes

Cooking Time: 10 minutes

Servings: 6

Ingredients: 2 cups un-sifted flour 2 teaspoons baking soda 1 teaspoon salt

3 tablespoons sugar 2 eggs 2⅓ cups low-fat buttermilk Butter for cooking

Directions:

Preheat a griddle or large skillet to 350°F.

Place a stick of butter next to the skillet; you will butter it before preparing each pancake.

In a medium bowl, whisk together the eggs and buttermilk until they are well combined. Whisk in the flour, baking soda, sugar, and salt. Whisk thoroughly until well combined.

Prepare the skillet by rubbing the butter in a circle in the center, then add about ½ cup of batter. Spread the batter until it forms an even circle.

When the pancake surface turns bubbly, flip and cook on the other side until you cannot see wet spots on the sides.

Repeat with the remaining batter, making sure to butter the skillet before you start each pancake. Serve with your favorite syrup or fruit.

Nutrition: Calories: 110, Total Fat: 6g, Total Carbohydrate: 34g, Protein: 6g

5.   Ham and Egg Casserole

Preparation Time: 10 minutes

Cooking Time: 10 minutes

Servings: 2

Ingredients: ⅓ cup lean ham (country cured is best)

1 slice sourdough bread, crust removed and cut to fit bottom of casserole dish

5 beaten eggs (about 1 cup) ¼ cup evaporated milk ¼ teaspoon salt

¼ teaspoon ground black pepper ¾ cup shredded mild cheddar cheese

Directions:

Prepare a casserole dish by spraying with nonstick cooking spray or greasing. Place the sourdough bread on the bottom. In a medium mixing bowl, beat together the eggs, salt, pepper, and evaporated milk. Stir until completely combined, then pour over the sourdough bread. Drop in the diced ham, then top with shredded cheese. Refrigerate for a couple of hours or preferably overnight.

Bake in an oven preheated to 350°F for 20–22 minutes or until set.

Nutrition: Calories: 212.7, Total Fat: 10.1 g, Saturated Fat: 4.9 g,

Cholesterol: 183.4 mg Sodium: 501.9 mg, Potassium: 220.0 mg,

Total Carbohydrate: 14.3 g, Dietary Fiber   : 1.1 g, Sugars: 1.9 g, Protein: 15.8 g

6. Sawmill Gravy and Biscuits

Preparation Time: 10 minutes

Cooking Time: 10 minutes

Servings: 4

Ingredients: ¼ cup sausage patty grease ¼ cup flour 1 sausage patty

½ cup bacon bits 2 cups milk ½ teaspoon salt ½ teaspoon coarsely ground pepper

Buttermilk biscuits for serving

Directions:

Add the sausage patty to a skillet and cook through. Remove from skillet and allow to cool, then crumble. Add the flour to the grease from the sausage in the skillet and stir until well combined.

Add the milk and cook while whisking constantly to avoid burning the milk. The gravy will thicken and bubble. Add the salt and pepper, crumbled sausage, and bacon bits.

Serve with your favorite buttermilk biscuits.

If you want to make a large batch of this gravy, you can use breakfast sausage chubs instead of a patty and crumble while you cook, then remove from the skillet and prepare the gravy the same way. You will need to increase the other ingredients proportionately, of course.

Nutrition: Calories: 754.0, Total Fat: 66.3 g, Saturated Fat: 25.3 g,

Cholesterol: 81.9 mg, Sodium   : 2,878.6 mg, Potassium: 219.4 mg,

Total Carbohydrate: 25.6 g, Dietary Fiber: 1.4 g, Sugars: 0.1 g,

Protein   12.6 g

7. Blueberry Syrup

Preparation Time: 5 minutes

Cooking Time: 20 minutes

Servings: 8

Ingredients:

2 cups blueberries ½ cup sugar 1 cup water 1 tablespoon cornstarch

Directions:

Combine the cornstarch with 2 tablespoons of water in a small bowl. Whisk until no longer clumpy and set aside.

Combine the water, blueberries, and sugar in a saucepan. Bring the mixture to a boil, then reduce the heat and simmer for about 10 minutes or until it has reduced a bit. Stir in the cornstarch and whisk until well combined. Continue to simmer and stir until the sauce has thickened.

When it has reached a syrup-like consistency, remove from heat. You can mix with an immersion blender if you choose.

Serve with pancakes or waffles.

Nutrition:

Calories: 45, Total Fat: 0.1g, Saturated Fat: 0g,   Cholesterol: 0mg,

Sodium: 0.7mg, Total Carbohydrate: 11.9g,   Dietary Fiber: 0.5g,

Sugars: 10.5g

8. Eggs-in-the-basket

Preparation Time: 12 minutes

Cooking Time: 3 minutes

Servings: 1

Ingredients:

1 slice of bread

1 teaspoon butter

1 large egg

Salt and pepper to taste

Directions:

Cut a 3-in. hole in the middle of the bread and discard. In a small skillet, melt the butter; place the bread in the skillet.

Place egg in the hole. Cook for about 2 minutes over medium heat until the bread is lightly browned. Turn and cook the other side until egg yolk is almost set. Season with salt and pepper.

Nutrition:

Calories: 183,

Fat: 10g, Cholesterol: 196mg, Sodium: 244mg,

Carbohydrate: 15g, Sugars: 2g, Fiber: 1g, 9g protein

9.   Avocado Eggrolls

Preparation Time: 10 minutes

Cooking Time: 15 minutes

Servings: 16

Ingredients:

For Filling:

4 avocados, peeled, pitted &

mashed ½ cup red onion, finely chopped

Juice of ½ a lemon or to taste

3 tablespoons sun dried tomatoes packed in oil, chopped

¼ cup cilantro, fresh, chopped 1 jalapeno, finely chopped Black pepper & salt to taste

For Cashew-Cilantro Sauce:

3 teaspoon white vinegar

½ teaspoon tamarind pulp 1 teaspoon balsamic vinegar

4 tablespoon brown sugar 1 cup fresh cilantro, chopped ½ cup cashews, chopped

3-4 garlic cloves ¼ cup red onion, chopped 1 tablespoon olive oil

3-4 tablespoon water Black pepper & salt to taste

Additional Ingredients:

1 tablespoon all-purpose flour or any of your favorite 16 egg roll wrappers

Oil for frying 1 tablespoons water

Directions:

For Filling:

Combine the entire ingredients together in a large bowl until combined well. Taste & adjust the amount of lemon juice, black pepper, or salt, if required; set aside until ready to use.

For Cashew-Cilantro Sauce:

Add the entire sauce ingredients together in a blender & blend on high power until completely smooth. Taste & adjust the amount of tang or sweetness per your preference.

To Assemble:

In a medium-sized bowl; combined flour with water until a sticky paste like consistency is formed. Now, lay an egg roll wrapper on a clean, flat surface. Put the filling in the middle & fold by sealing the edges using a flour-water mix.

Get the other egg rolls ready in the similar pattern.

Now, over moderate heat in a deep pot; heat up the oil until hot. Once done; work in batches and add a few egg rolls into the hot oil; fry for a couple of minutes, until turn golden & crispy.

Serve warm with the prepared sauce on side. Enjoy.

Nutrition:

Calories: 1060, Total Fat: 65 g,

Cholesterol: 74 mg, Sodium: 1583 mg, Total Carbohydrate: 107 g,

Dietary Fiber: 19 g, Sugar: 23 g, Protein: 16 g

10. Harvest Grain 'N Nut" Pancakes

Preparation Time: 5 minutes

Cooking Time: 5 minutes

Servings: 4

Ingredients: 1 teaspoon olive oil ¾ cup oats, powdered ¾ cup whole wheat flour

2 teaspoons baking soda 1 teaspoon baking powder ½ teaspoon salt

½ cup buttermilk ¼ cup vegetable oil 1 egg ¼ cup sugar

3 tablespoons almonds, finely sliced 3 tablespoons walnuts, sliced

Syrup for serving

Directions: Heat oil in a pan over medium heat.

As pan preheats, pulverize oats in a blender until powdered. Then, add to a large bowl with flour, baking soda, baking powder and salt. Mix well. Add buttermilk, oil, egg, and sugar in a separate bowl. Mix with an electric mixer until creamy. Mix in wet ingredients with dry ingredients, then add nuts. Mix everything together with electric mixer.

Scoop ⅓ cup of batter and cook in the hot pan for at least 2 minutes or until both sides turn golden brown. Transfer onto a plate, then repeat for the remaining batter.

Serve with syrup.

Nutrition: Calories 433, Total Fat 24 g, Carbohydrates 46 g, Protein 12 g,

Sodium 1128 mg

11. Cinnamon Apples

Preparation Time: 10 minutes

Cooking Time: 10 minutes

Servings: 4

Ingredients: ¼ cup butter ½ cup apple cider 1 tablespoon cornstarch

2 pounds Golden Delicious apples, cored, peeled, and cut into wedges

1 teaspoon lemon juice 1 teaspoon cinnamon ⅛ teaspoon nutmeg

⅛ teaspoon allspice ¼ cup brown sugar

Directions:

In a large skillet, melt your butter over a medium to medium-low heat. Add the apples in a single layer, and then top with the lemon juice followed by the brown sugar and spices. Cover reduce the heat to low and allow the apples to simmer until tender.

Transfer the apples from the skillet to a serving bowl, leaving the juices in the skillet.

Whisk ½ cup of the juice together with the cornstarch in a small bowl. Turn the heat under the skillet up to medium-high and whisk the cornstarch mixture into the rest of the juices. Stir constantly until it thickens and there are no lumps.

Pour the juice over the bowl of apples and stir to coat.

Nutrition: Calories: 128, Fat: 2g, Protein: 0.3g, Carbohydrate: 29.2g, Fiber: 1.3g, Cholesterol: 5mg, Iron: 0.6mg, Sodium: 21mg, Calcium: 25mg

12. Cheese 'n' Grits Casserole

Preparation Time: 10 minutes

Cooking Time: 10 minutes

Servings: 8

Ingredients: 4 cups water 1 cup uncooked old-fashioned grits

1/2 teaspoon salt 1/2 cup 2% milk 1/4 cup butter, melted

2 large eggs, lightly beaten 1 cup shredded cheddar cheese

1 tablespoon Worcestershire sauce 1/8 teaspoon cayenne pepper

1/8 teaspoon paprika

Directions:

Preheat oven to 350°. In a large saucepan, bring water to a boil.

Slowly stir in grits and salt. Reduce heat; cover and simmer until thickened, 5-7 minutes.

Cool slightly.

Gradually whisk in milk, butter, and eggs. Stir in cheese, Worcestershire sauce and cayenne.

Transfer to a greased 2-qt. baking dish. Sprinkle with paprika.

Bake, uncovered, until bubbly, 30-35 minutes. Let stand 10 minutes before serving.

Nutrition:

Calories: 202, Fat: 12g, Cholesterol: 86mg, Sodium: 335mg, Carbohydrate: 17g,

Protein: 7g

13. Deluxe Mashed Potatoes

Preparation Time: 30 minutes

Cooking Time: 35 minutes

Servings: 6

Ingredients:

4 to 5 large potatoes (about 2-1/2 pounds) 3 ounces cream cheese, softened

1/2 cup sour cream 1 tablespoon chopped chives 3/4 teaspoon onion salt

1/4 teaspoon pepper 1 tablespoon butter Paprika, optional

Directions:

Peel and cube the potatoes, place in a saucepan and cover with water.

Cook over medium heat until tender; drain.

Mash until smooth (do not add milk or butter).

Stir in cream cheese, sour cream, chives, onion salt and pepper.

Spoon into a greased 1-1/2-qt. baking dish.

Dot with butter; sprinkle with paprika if desired.

Cover and bake at 350° for 35-40 minutes or until heated through.

Nutrition:

Calories: 301, Fat: 10g, Cholesterol: 34mg, Sodium: 313mg, Carbohydrate: 45g, Protein: 7g

14. Sausage Egg Muffin

Preparation Time: 10 minutes

Cooking Time: 15 minutes

Servings: 4

Ingredients: 4 English muffins, cut in half horizontally

4 slices American processed cheese ½ tablespoon oil 1-pound ground pork, minced

½ teaspoon dried sage, ground ½ teaspoon dried thyme 1 teaspoon onion powder

¾ teaspoon black pepper ¾ teaspoon salt ½ teaspoon white sugar

4 large ⅓-inch onion ring slices 4 large eggs 2 tablespoons water

Directions: Preheat oven to 300°F. Cover one-half of muffin with cheese, leaving one half uncovered. Transfer both halves to a baking tray. Place in oven. For the sausage patties, use your hands to mix pork, sage, thyme, onion powder, pepper, salt, and sugar in a bowl. Form into 4 patties. Make sure they are slightly larger than the muffins. Heat oil in a pan. Cook patties on both sides for at least 2 minutes each or until all sides turn brown. Remove tray of muffins from oven. Place cooked sausage patties on top of the cheese on muffins. Return tray to the oven. In the same pan, position onion rings flat into a single layer. Crack one egg inside each of the onion rings to make them round. Add water carefully into the sides of the pan and cover. Cook for 2 minutes. Remove tray of muffins from the oven. Add eggs on top of patties, then top with the other muffin half.

Serve warm.

Nutrition: Calories: 453, Total Fat: 15 g, Carbohydrates: 67 g, Protein: 15 g,

Sodium: 1008 mg

Chapter 2 Sides and Salads

15. Coleslaw

Preparation Time: 10 minutes

Cooking Time: 3 hours

Servings: 4

Ingredients:

2 cups shredded cabbage

½ cup shredded carrots

½ cup shredded purple cabbage

1 cup Miracle Whip

1 teaspoon celery seeds

½ teaspoon salt

½ teaspoon pepper

⅓ cup sugar

¼ cup vinegar

¼ cup buttermilk

¼ cup milk

4 teaspoons lemon juice

Directions:

Toss the carrots and cabbages in a large mixing bowl.

Stir in the Miracle Whip, celery seeds, salt, pepper, sugar, vinegar, buttermilk, milk, and lemon juice. Toss again to completely combine.

Refrigerate for about 3 hours before serving.

Nutrition:

Calories: 156.5,

Total Fat: 10.5 g,

Saturated Fat: 1.6 g, Cholesterol: 14.5 mg,

Sodium: 1,457.4 mg, Potassium: 263.0 mg,

Total Carbohydrate: 14.4 g, Dietary Fiber: 2.2 g,

Sugars: 6.5 g, Protein   1.8 g

16. Green Beans

Preparation Time: 5 minutes

Cooking Time: 35 minutes

Servings: 4

Ingredients: 4 slices thick-cut bacon, chopped into pieces

1 (14½-ounce) can cut green beans in water (do not drain) ½ cup onion, finely diced

1 teaspoon sugar Salt Pepper

Directions:

Add the bacon to a large saucepan and cook over medium heat until it is browned but not yet crispy.

Stir in the green beans (with liquid), onion and sugar. Bring to a boil, then reduce heat and simmer for 30–35 minutes.

Season to taste and serve.

Nutrition:

Calories: 155.3, Total Fat: 9 g, Saturated Fat: 2.9 g, Cholesterol: 12.8 mg,

Sodium: 363.8 mg, Total Carbohydrate: 15.7 g, Dietary Fiber: 5.7 g,

Sugars: 7.6 g, Protein: 6 g

17. Brussels Sprout N' Kale Salad

Preparation Time: 5 minutes

Cooking Time: 1 minute

Servings: 4 to 6

Ingredients: 1 bunch kale 1-pound Brussels sprouts

¼ cup craisins (or dry cranberries) ½ cup pecans, chopped

Maple vinaigrette

½ cup olive oil ¼ cup apple cider vinegar ¼ cup maple syrup 1 teaspoon dry mustard

Directions:

Slice the kale and Brussels sprouts with a cheese grater or mandolin slicer. Transfer to a salad bowl.

Add the pecans to a skillet on high heat. Toast for 60 seconds, then transfer to the salad bowl. Add the craisins. Mix together all of the ingredients for the vinaigrette and whisk to combine. Pour the vinaigrette over the salad and toss. Refrigerate for a few hours or preferably overnight before serving.

Nutrition: Calories 280, Total Fat 20g, Saturated Fat 2g, Trans Fat 0g,

Cholesterol 0mg, Sodium 180mg, Total Carbohydrates 33g, Dietary Fiber 4g,

Sugars 25g, Protein 3g

18. Chicken Pot stickers

Preparation Time: 40 minutes

Cooking Time: 30 minutes

Servings: 50

Ingredients:

½ cup + 2 tablespoons soy sauce, divided 1 tablespoon rice vinegar

3 tablespoons chives, divided 1 tablespoon sesame seeds 1 teaspoon sriracha hot sauce

1-pound ground pork 3 cloves garlic, minced 1 egg, beaten 1½ tablespoons sesame oil

1 tablespoon fresh ginger, minced 50 dumpling wrappers 1 cup vegetable oil, for frying

1-quart water

Directions:

In a mixing bowl, whisk together the ½ cup of soy sauce, vinegar, 1 tablespoon of the chives, sesame seeds and sriracha to make the dipping sauce. In a separate bowl, mix together the pork, garlic, egg, the rest of the chives, the 2 tablespoons of soy sauce, sesame oil and the ginger. Add about 1 tablespoon of the filling to each dumpling wrapper. Pinch the sides of the wrappers together to seal. You may need to wet the edges a bit, so they will stick. Heat the cup of oil in a large skillet. When hot, working in batches, add the dumplings and cook until golden brown on all sides. Take care of not overloading your pan. Add the water and cook until tender, then serve with the dipping sauce.

Nutrition: Calories: 140, Total Fat: 5 g, Cholesterol: 15 mg, Sodium : 470 mg

Total Carbohydrate: 19 g, Dietary Fiber: 1 g, Sugar: 2 g,   Protein   6 g

19. Lettuce Wraps

Preparation Time: 10 minutes

Cooking Time: 10 minutes

Servings: 4

Ingredients: 1 tablespoon olive oil 1-pound ground chicken 2 cloves garlic, minced

1 onion, diced ¼ cup hoisin sauce 2 tablespoons soy sauce

1 tablespoon rice wine vinegar 1 tablespoon ginger, freshly grated

1 tablespoon Sriracha (optional)

1 (8-ounce) can whole water chestnuts, drained and diced 2 green onions, thinly sliced

Kosher salt and freshly ground black pepper to taste 1 head iceberg lettuce

Directions:

Add the oil to a deep skillet or saucepan and heat over medium-high heat.

When hot, add the chicken and cook until it is completely cooked through.

Stir while cooking to make sure it is properly crumbled.

Drain any excess fat from the skillet, then add the garlic, onion, hoisin sauce, soy sauce, ginger, sriracha and vinegar.

Cook until the onions have softened, then stir in the water chestnuts and green onion and cook for another minute or so. Add salt and pepper to taste. Serve with lettuce leaves and eat by wrapping them up like a taco.

Nutrition: Calories: 157, Fat: 8 g, Cholesterol: 0 mg, Protein: 15.7 g,

Carbohydrates: 10.5 g, Sugar: 2.7 g, Fiber: 1.9 g

20. Shrimp Dumplings

Preparation Time: 20 minutes

Cooking Time: 10 minutes

Servings: 4 to 6

Ingredients: 1-pound medium shrimp, peeled, deveined, washed, and dried, divided

2 tablespoons carrot, finely minced 2 tablespoons green onion, finely minced

1 teaspoon ginger, freshly minced 2 tablespoons oyster sauce

¼ teaspoon sesame oil 1 package wonton wrappers

Sauce 1 cup soy sauce 2 tablespoons white vinegar ½ teaspoon chili paste

2 tablespoons granulated sugar ½ teaspoon ginger, freshly minced

Sesame oil to taste 1 cup water 1 tablespoon cilantro leaves

Directions: In a food processor or blender, finely mince ½ pound of the shrimp. Dice the other ½ pound of shrimp. In a mixing bowl, combine both the minced and diced shrimp with the remaining ingredients. Spoon about 1 teaspoon of the mixture into each wonton wrapper. Wet the edges of the wrapper with your finger, then fold up and seal tightly. Cover and refrigerate for at least an hour. In a medium bowl, combine all of the ingredients for the sauce and stir until well combined. When ready to serve, boil water in a saucepan and cover with a steamer. You may want to lightly oil the steamer to keep the dumplings from sticking. Steam the dumplings for 7–10 minutes.

Serve with sauce.

Nutrition: Calories: 190, Total Fat: 4 g, Cholesterol: 118 mg, Sodium: 890 mg,

Total Carbohydrate: 20 g, Dietary Fiber: 0 g, Sugar: 4 g,   Protein: 17 g

21. Dry Garlic Ribs

Preparation Time: 15 minutes

Cooking Time: 2 hours and 30 minutes

Servings: 4 to 6

Ingredients:

6 pounds pork ribs, silver skin removed and cut into individual ribs 1½ cups broth

1½ cups brown sugar ¼ cup soy sauce 12 cloves garlic, minced

¼ cup yellow mustard 1 large onion, finely chopped ¼ teaspoon salt

½ teaspoon black pepper

Directions:

Preheat oven to 200°F. Season ribs with salt and pepper and place on a baking tray. Cover with aluminum foil and bake for 1 hour.

In a mixing bowl, stir together the broth, brown sugar, soy sauce, garlic, mustard, and onion. Continue stirring until the sugar is completely dissolved.

After an hour, remove the foil from the ribs and turn the heat up to 350°F.

Carefully pour the sauce over the ribs. Re-cover with the foil and return to the oven for 1 hour.

Remove the foil and bake for 15 more minutes on each side.

Nutrition: Calories: 210, Total Fat: 13g Cholesterol: 70mg, Sodium: 480mg,

Potassium: 0mg, Total Carbohydrate: 3g, Dietary Fiber: 0g, Sugar: 0g,

Protein: 20g

22. Stuffed Mushrooms

Preparation Time: 10 minutes

Cooking Time: 30 minutes

Servings: 4

Ingredients: 1 tablespoon Romano cheese, finely grated

9 ounces mushrooms 6 ounces clams, drained 1 tablespoon green onion, chopped fine

1 egg, beaten ½ teaspoon garlic, minced ⅛ teaspoon garlic salt

½ cup Italian breadcrumbs 1 teaspoon oregano leaves

1 tablespoon butter, melted and cooled 2 tablespoons parmesan cheese, finely grated

2 tablespoons mozzarella cheese, finely grated (for stuffing)

¼ cup mozzarella cheese, finely grated (for garnish) ¼ cup butter, melted

Directions: Remove stems and wash mushrooms. Pat dry. Drain the clams. Set aside the stems and clam juice for later. Preheat oven to 350°F. Place clams, onions, garlic salt, minced garlic, cooled butter, and oregano in a bowl. Mix together, then add cheeses, breadcrumbs, egg, and clam juice. Mix well to make clam stuffing. Stuff each mushroom with clam stuffing, making a mound. Place the mushrooms in a baking dish and pour the melted butter over them. Cover the baking dish with foil. Place in oven and bake for about 35–40 minutes. Remove the foil and sprinkle mozzarella cheese on top. Return to the oven until cheese is melted. Garnish by sprinkling with freshly diced parsley. Serve.

Nutrition: Calories: 50, Total Fat 3g, Saturated Fat 0.5g, Cholesterol 10mg,

Sodium 85mg, Total Carbohydrate 3g, Dietary Fiber 1g, Total Sugars 1g, Protein 4g

23. Spinach Artichoke Dip

Preparation Time: 15 minutes

Cooking Time: 10 minutes

Servings: 8

Ingredients Salt and pepper to taste 3 tablespoons butter 3 tablespoons flour

1½ cups milk ½ teaspoon salt ¼ teaspoon black pepper

5 ounces spinach, frozen and chopped

¼ cup artichokes, diced (I personally like to use marinated)

½ teaspoon garlic, chopped ½ cup parmesan, shredded ½ cup mozzarella, shredded

1 tablespoon asiago cheese, shredded 1 tablespoon Romano cheese, shredded

2 tablespoons cream cheese ¼ cup mozzarella cheese (for topping)

Directions:

Melt butter over medium heat in a saucepan. Add flour and cook for about 1–2 minutes. Add milk and stir until thick. Season with salt and pepper to taste. Add spinach, diced artichokes, garlic, cheeses, and cream cheese to the pan. Stir until warmed.

Pour into a small baking dish. Sprinkle mozzarella cheese on top and place under the broiler. Broil until the top begins browning.

Nutrition: Calories 100, Total Fat: 9 g, Cholesterol: 15 mg,

Sodium   220 mg, Total Carbohydrate: 1 g, Dietary Fiber 0 g, Sugars   0 g,

Protein   4 g

24. Clams Bruschetta

Preparation Time: 15 minutes

Cooking Time: 2 minutes

Servings: 4 to 8

Ingredients:

8 slices Italian bread

1 clove garlic, halved ½ cup extra virgin olive oil

1 cup (or 2 6-ounce cans) chopped clam meat, drained

4 large ripe tomatoes, cut into thick slices Salt and freshly ground pepper to taste

12 fresh arugula or basil leaves, rinsed and dried

Directions:

Preheat grill, then toast both sides of the bread slices.

Rub the garlic onto each side of the bread to infuse with flavor.

Place a tomato slice and some clam meat on each bread slice. Sprinkle with salt and pepper to taste. Drizzle olive oil on top.

Cut arugula or basil thinly and place onto bruschetta. Serve.

Nutrition:

Calories: 424.4. Total Fat 29.4 g, Cholesterol 19.3 mg, Sodium 276.8 mg,

Total Carbohydrate 29.1 g, Dietary Fiber 3.4 g, Sugar: 5.2 g, Protein 12.6 g

25. Fried Mozzarella

Preparation Time: 10 minutes

Cooking Time: 10 minutes

Servings: 4

Ingredients

1-pound mozzarella or other cheese 2 eggs, beaten ¼ cup water

1½ cups Italian breadcrumbs ½ teaspoons garlic salt 1 teaspoon Italian seasoning

⅔ cup flour ⅓ cup cornstarch

Directions

Make thick cuts of the cheese. In a bowl, make an egg wash by beating together eggs and water. In another bowl, mix the breadcrumbs, garlic salt, and Italian seasoning. In a third bowl, mix together flour and cornstarch.

Heat vegetable oil in a frying pan.

Dip each piece of cheese into the flour, then egg wash, then breadcrumbs. Fry until golden brown. Remove from oil and drain on paper towel. Serve with marinara sauce.

Nutrition:

Calories 682, Total Fat 40 g, Cholesterol 79 mg, Sodium 1,325 mg, Potassium 222 mg,

Total Carbohydrate 50 g,

Dietary fiber 3.8 g, Sugar 3.4 g,

Protein 32 g

26. Hot n' Spicy Buffalo Wings

Preparation Time: 15 minutes

Cooking Time: 12 minutes

Servings: 2

Ingredients:

½ cup flour ¼ teaspoon paprika ¼ teaspoon cayenne pepper ¼ teaspoon salt

10 chicken wings Vegetable oil, for deep-frying

¼ cup butter ¼ cup Louisiana hot sauce 1 dash ground black pepper

1 dash garlic powder Blue cheese salad dressing Celery cut into sticks

Directions:

In a bowl, add flour, paprika, cayenne pepper, and salt. Mix well. In a separate bowl, add chicken wings. Lightly coat with flour mixture. Make sure the coating for each wing is even. Refrigerate for at least 1 hour to keep the coating attached while frying. To prepare, preheat about 1½-inch deep oil in deep fryer to 375°F. In a separate small pot, heat butter, hot sauce, pepper, and garlic powder. Stir until butter is dissolved and ingredients are well mixed. Carefully lower coated chicken wings into the hot oil. Deep fry for about 10 to 15 minutes or until wings turns partly dark brown then transfer onto a plate lined with paper towels to drain. While the wings are still hot, transfer to a bowl and pour hot sauce mixture on top. Toss to coat all wings evenly. Serve hot with blue cheese dressing and celery sticks.

Nutrition:

Calories: 867, Total fat: 63 g, Saturated fat: 26 g, Carbohydrates: 25 g,

Sugar: 1 g, Fibers: 1 g, Protein: 49 g, Sodium: 1419 mg

27. Guacamole

Preparation Time: 10 minutes

Cooking Time: 0 minutes

Servings: 10

Ingredients:

1 medium jalapeño pepper, seeded and deveined, finely chopped

1 cup fresh red onion, finely diced

2 tablespoons fresh cilantro, chopped finely

8 ripe avocados

8 teaspoons freshly squeezed lime juice

1 teaspoon kosher salt

Directions:

Halve avocados using a knife and remove pits and spoon flesh into a large bowl. Add jalapeño pepper, onion, and cilantro. Pour in the lime juice. Sprinkle salt on top. Mash avocado with the rest of the ingredients until everything is well blended and desired consistency is obtained.

Cover guacamole with plastic wrap until just before serving.

Nutrition:

Calories: 233, Total fat: 21 g, Saturated fat: 3 g, Carbohydrates: 12 g,

Sugar: 1 g, Fibers: 10 g, Protein: 3 g, Sodium: 243 mg

28. Loaded Potato Skins

Preparation Time: 30 minutes

Cooking Time: 7 minutes

Servings: 6

Ingredients:

1 teaspoon oil 6 medium-sized potatoes 1 cup vegetable oil

8 ounces Cheddar cheese, grated 3 strips thick cut cooked bacon, diced

16 ounces sour cream 1 ripe tomato, diced

Fresh chives for serving, chopped finely

Directions:

Preheat oven to 375°F. Line a large baking sheet with parchment paper. Using a fork, prick potatoes in a few places. Microwave for at least 10 minutes or until soft. Halve the potatoes vertically and remove the insides of the potato until there is only ¼ inch of the potato shell left. In a deep saucepan, heat oil to 365 °F. Deep-fry potato shells for 5 minutes, then transfer onto plate lined with paper towels.

Add cheese and diced bacon into potato shells. Place on the baking sheet prepared earlier and bake for at least 7 minutes or until cheese is fully melted.

Serve immediately with spoonful of sour cream on top or on the side. Sprinkle with diced tomatoes and chives.

Nutrition:

Calories: 519, Total Fat: 33 g, Carbohydrates: 41 g, Protein 17 g,

Sodium 361 mg

Chapter 3 Poultry and Fish

29. Grilled Chicken Tenderloins

Preparation Time: 10 minutes

Cooking Time: 1 hour 10 minutes

Servings: 4

Ingredients:

1 lb. chicken tenders or cut chicken breasts

1/2 cup Italian dressing

2 tablespoons honey

2 teaspoons lime juice

Directions:

Place chicken tenderloins into a large plastic bag with wet ingredients.

Marinate in refrigerator for at least one hour.

Add chicken and liquid to a large skillet.

Cook over medium heat until liquid is reduced, and chicken is golden in color, but not dry.

Be sure to turn chicken throughout the cooking process.

Nutrition:

Calories: 201,

Carbohydrates: 3g,

Protein: 24g,

Fat: 9g

Saturated Fat: 1g,

Cholesterol: 72mg,

Sodium: 423mg,

Potassium: 444mg,

Sugar: 3g

30. Sunday Fried Chicken

Preparation Time: 10 minutes

Cooking Time: 20 minutes

Servings: 4

Ingredients:

oil for frying 4 boneless, skinless chicken breasts 2 cups all-purpose flour

2 teaspoons salt 2 teaspoons ground black pepper 1 cup buttermilk 1/2 cup water

Directions:

Pour 3 to 4 inches of oil into a deep fryer or large pot and preheat the oil to 350 degrees. Prepare seasoned flour by combining the flour, salt, and pepper in a bowl. Stir to combine well. In another bowl mix together the buttermilk and water. If your chicken breasts are not fairly uniform in size place them between two pieces of wax paper and gently pound them out with a meat pounder until they are more uniform in size. This will help with even cooking times. Pat chicken breasts dry with a paper towel. Season the chicken with salt and pepper and then dredge into the flour, dip in buttermilk, and then dredge again in the seasoned flour and deep-fry the chicken pieces in the hot oil.

Turn the chicken breasts during the cooking to make sure that both sides of the chicken are golden brown. This should take 7 to 8 minutes for each one to cook.

When the chicken is done, drain in a wire rack.

Nutrition:

Calories: 503, Carbohydrates: 51g, Protein: 8g, Fat: 29g, Saturated Fat: 23g,

Cholesterol: 7mg, Sodium: 1229mg, Potassium: 161mg, Fiber: 1g, Sugar: 3g

31. Broccoli Cheddar Chicken

Preparation Time: 10 minutes

Cooking Time: 45 minutes

Servings: 4

Ingredients:

4 boneless skinless chicken breasts 1 can of Campbell's Cheddar Cheese Soup

1 cup milk 1 1/2 cups Ritz Crackers (one sleeve)

4 tablespoons of melted butter (you can use more) 8 ounces frozen broccoli

4 ounces shredded cheddar cheese 1/2 teaspoon seasoned salt

Directions:

Preheat your oven to 350 degrees. Make can of Cheddar cheese soup mix according to package directions (one can of soup mix to one can of milk). Place chicken breasts in a 9 by 13-inch baking dish. Season with seasoned salt. Pour 3/4 of the prepared soup over the chicken breasts. Add broccoli to chicken that has been covered with the cheddar soup. Melt butter and combine with Ritz crackers, sprinkle buttered crackers over the broccoli. Add remaining soup mix and bake for approximately 45 minutes or until the chicken is done. (Check chicken by cutting the thickest part and look to see that the chicken is uniform in color).

When chicken has been removed from oven sprinkle with shredded cheddar cheese.

Nutrition:

Calories: 1354, Carbohydrates: 91g, Protein: 86g, Fat: 67g, Saturated Fat: 30g,

Cholesterol: 281mg, Sodium: 5234mg, Potassium: 4924mg, Fiber: 8g, Sugar: 20g

32. Old Country Store Dumplings

Preparation Time: 20 minutes

Cooking Time: 20 minutes

Servings: 4

Ingredients:

Dumplings

2 cups all-purpose flour, plus more for kneading and rolling

2 teaspoons baking powder 1/2 teaspoon salt 1 cup whole milk

1/4 cup vegetable oil 2 quarts water

3 chicken bouillon cubes or about 2 teaspoons of soup base

Sauce

3 tablespoons butterSalt to taste1/4 cup all-purpose flour

1/2 teaspoon sugar1 cup buttermilk or whole milk

2 chicken bouillon cubes, crumbled or about 2 teaspoons chicken soup base

1/2 to 3/4 cup dumpling cooking liquid (from after dumplings have been cooked)

Directions:

Dumplings

Mix the flour, baking powder, salt, milk, and oil, blending well, and turn out onto a floured surface.

Knead four or five times.

Divide the dough into two pieces.

Roll out one piece to 1/8-inch thick and cut into 1 x 1 1/2-inch dumplings.

In a large saucepan, combine the water and bouillon cubes/soup base.

Boil until the bouillon cubes/soup base dissolve.

Cook half of the dumplings until just about done; dumplings are done when they float up towards the top of the pot. Use a strainer to remove them to a bowl and set aside.

Finish the other half of the dumplings in the same way. Reserve the cooking liquid.

Sauce

While the dumplings are cooking, you can start to prepare the sauce.

Melt the butter in medium saucepan. Add salt and flour; stir until thick.

Mix the sugar with the milk and add to flour mixture a little at a time, stirring constantly with a whisk until thick and smooth. Remove from heat.

Add the cooked dumplings to the sauce.

Dissolve the crumbled bouillon cubes in 1/2 cup of the cooking liquid and stir gently into the sauce and dumplings.

Return to low heat and simmer until blended. If the sauce seems too thick, gently stir in a little more cooking liquid.

Nutrition:

Calories: 529, Carbohydrates: 61g, Protein: 11g, Fat: 26g, Saturated Fat: 18g,

Cholesterol: 35mg, Sodium: 1363mg, Potassium: 430mg, Fiber: 1g,

Sugar: 6g

33. Chicken and Dumplings

Preparation Time: 30 minutes

Cooking Time: 1 hour 40 minutes

Servings: 6

Ingredients:

1 whole chicken, about 3 1/2 pounds

5 carrots

2 medium onions

5 celery stalks

2 bay leaves

4 stalks fresh parsley or 2 tablespoons dry flakes

1 teaspoon poultry seasoning

1 teaspoon salt

1/2 teaspoon freshly ground black pepper

2 1/2 cups flour

3 teaspoons baking powder

1 teaspoon salt

3 tablespoons solid shortening or butter, softened

1 1/4 cup milk

Directions:

Place chicken into a large Dutch oven and add 3 quarts water, or to cover. Around the chicken, arrange 3 carrots, one onion and 4 of the celery stalks, all roughly chopped. Add bay leaves, half the parsley, and the spices. Bring to a boil and then lower heat to a gentle simmer and cook 45 minutes. Chicken should be completely cooked – check to see that it is ready to fall off the bone and cook longer if necessary.

Remove chicken to a cutting board and strain liquid through a wire sieve over a large bowl. Measure 3 cups of the stock to use now and store any extra for another use.

Remove bones and skin from the chicken and shred all of the meat into bite-size pieces. Place chicken in the same Dutch oven, return the 3 cups of stock plus the remaining carrots, onion, and celery, all finely diced. Taste and add additional salt and pepper if desired. Simmer for 20 minutes while preparing the dumpling dough.

In a medium bowl, stir flour, baking powder and salt together, then use a pastry blender to add the shortening or butter until well mixed. Add remaining parsley, finely chopped, and stir in the milk to form a soft dough. Using a large spoon or 2-inch ice cream scoop, drop 12 spoonsful of dough on top of the simmering chicken mixture. Cook at a simmer for 5 minutes, then cover the pan and continue to simmer for 20 minutes.

Nutrition:

Calories 384,

Total fat: 15.2 g,

Cholesterol: 61 mg,

Sodium: 128 mg,

Carbohydrates: 35.3 g,

Protein: 25.7 g

34. Chicken Casserole

Preparation Time: 10 minutes

Cooking Time: 1 hour 5 minutes

Servings: 4

Ingredients:

Cornbread

1 cup yellow cornmeal 1/3 cup all-purpose flour 1 1/2 teaspoon baking powder

1 tablespoon sugar 1/2 teaspoon salt 1/2 teaspoon baking soda

2 tablespoons vegetable oil 3/4 cup buttermilk 1 egg 1/2 cup melted butter

Chicken Filling

2 tablespoons butter 1/4 cup chopped yellow onion 1/2 cup celery, thinly sliced

1 3/4 cup chicken broth 1 can cream of chicken soup

1 teaspoon salt 1/4 teaspoon pepper

2 1/2 cups cooked chicken breast, cut in bite-size pieces

Directions:

Cornbread

Mix all the ingredients for the cornbread except the melted butter together in a mixing bowl until smooth.

Pour the batter into a greased 8-inch square baking pan and bake at 375 degrees F for 20 - 25 minutes or until golden and done. Remove from the oven and let cool completely.

When the cornbread is cool, crumble all the cornbread and place 3 cups of the cornbread crumbs in a mixing bowl.

Add the 1/2 cup melted butter to crumbs and mix well, set aside.

Chicken Filling

In medium-sized saucepan on medium-low heat, heat the butter and sauté the chopped onions and celery until they are transparent, stirring occasionally.

Add the chicken broth, cream of chicken soup, salt, and pepper. Stir until well blended and the soup is dissolved completely.

Add the cooked chicken; stir and blend until mixture reaches a low simmer. Cook for 5 minutes, then remove from the heat.

Place the chicken filling in a buttered 2 1/2-quart casserole dish or individual casserole dishes (about four).

Sprinkle the cornbread crumb topping on top of the chicken mixture; do not stir into the chicken filling. It should form a crust over the filling.

Place the baking dish in preheated oven at 350 degrees F for 35 - 40 minutes. The crumbs will turn a golden yellow.

Serve while hot.

Nutrition:

Calories: 582, Carbohydrates: 50g, Protein: 37g,

Fat: 25g, Saturated Fat: 13g, Cholesterol: 141mg,

Sodium: 2111mg, Potassium: 757mg, Fiber: 4g, Sugar: 6g

35. Chicken-Fried Steak & Gravy

Preparation Time: 15 minutes

Cooking Time: 10 minutes

Servings: 4

Ingredients: 1-1/4 cups all-purpose flour, divided 2 large eggs

1-1/2 cups 2% milk, divided 4 beef cube steaks (6 ounces each)

1-1/4 teaspoons salt, divided 1 teaspoon pepper, divided

Oil for frying 1 cup water

Directions:

Place 1 cup flour in a shallow bowl. In a separate shallow bowl, whisk eggs and 1/2 cup milk until blended. Sprinkle steaks with 3/4 teaspoon each salt and pepper. Dip in flour to coat both sides; shake off excess. Dip in egg mixture, then again in flour.

In a large cast-iron or other heavy skillet, heat 1/4 in. of oil over medium heat. Add steaks; cook until golden brown and a thermometer reads 160°, 4-6 minutes on each side. Remove from pan; drain on paper towels. Keep warm.

Remove all but 2 tablespoons oil from pan. Stir in the remaining 1/4 cup flour, 1/2 teaspoon salt and 1/4 teaspoon pepper until smooth; cook and stir over medium heat until golden brown, 3-4 minutes. Gradually whisk in water and remaining milk. Bring to a boil, stirring constantly; cook and stir until thickened, 1-2 minutes. Serve with steaks.

Nutrition: Calories: 563, Fat: 28g, Saturated fat: 5g, Cholesterol: 148mg,

Sodium: 839mg, Carbohydrate: 29g, Sugars: 4g Fiber: 1g, Protein: 46g

36. Spicy Oven-Fried Chicken

Preparation Time: 25 minutes

Cooking Time: 35 minutes

Servings: 8

Ingredients:

8 bone-in chicken breast halves, skin removed (8 ounces each) 2 cups buttermilk

2 tablespoons Dijon mustard 2 teaspoons salt 2 teaspoons hot pepper sauce

1-1/2 teaspoons garlic powder 2 cups soft breadcrumbs 1 cup cornmeal

2 tablespoons canola oil 1/2 teaspoon poultry seasoning 1/2 teaspoon ground mustard

1/2 teaspoon paprika 1/2 teaspoon cayenne pepper 1/4 teaspoon dried oregano

1/4 teaspoon dried parsley flakes

Directions:

Preheat oven to 400°. In a large bowl or dish, combine the first five ingredients. Add chicken and turn to coat. Refrigerate 1 hour or overnight. Drain chicken, discarding marinade. In a large bowl, combine remaining ingredients.

Add chicken, one piece at a time, and coat with crumb mixture.

Place on a parchment-lined baking sheet. Bake 35-40 minutes or until a thermometer reads 170°.

Nutrition:

Calories: 296, Fat: 7g, Cholesterol: 103mg, Sodium: 523mg, Carbohydrate: 15g

Protein: 40g

37. Skillet-Grilled Catfish

Preparation Time: 15 minutes

Cooking Time: 10 minutes

Servings: 4

Ingredients: 1/4 cup all-purpose flour 1/4 cup cornmeal

1 teaspoon onion powder 1 teaspoon dried basil 1/2 teaspoon garlic salt

1/2 teaspoon dried thyme 1/4 to 1/2 teaspoon white pepper

1/4 to 1/2 teaspoon cayenne pepper 1/4 to 1/2 teaspoon pepper

4 catfish fillets (6 to 8 ounces each) 1/4 cup butter

Directions:

In a large shallow dish, combine the first 9 ingredients.

Add catfish, one fillet at a time, and turn to coat.

Place a large cast-iron skillet on a grill rack over medium-high heat.

Melt butter in the skillet; add catfish in batches, if necessary.

Grill, covered, until fish just begins to flake easily with a fork, 5-10 minutes on each side.

Nutrition:

Calories: 222, Fat: 15g, Cholesterol: 51mg, Sodium: 366mg, Carbohydrate: 14g,

Protein: 8g

38. Country Chicken with Gravy

Preparation Time: 5 minutes

Cooking Time: 25 minutes

Servings: 4

Ingredients: 3/4 cup crushed cornflakes 1/2 teaspoon poultry seasoning

1/2 teaspoon paprika 1/4 teaspoon salt 1/4 teaspoon dried thyme

1/4 teaspoon pepper 2 tablespoons fat-free evaporated milk

4 boneless skinless chicken breast halves (4 ounces each) 2 teaspoons canola oil

Gravy:

1 tablespoon butter 1 tablespoon all-purpose flour 1/4 teaspoon pepper

1/8 teaspoon salt 1/2 cup fat-free evaporated milk

1/4 cup condensed chicken broth, undiluted

1 teaspoon sherry or additional condensed chicken broth 2 tablespoons minced chives

Directions: In a shallow bowl, combine the first six ingredients. Place milk in another shallow bowl. Dip chicken in milk, then roll in cornflake mixture. In a large nonstick skillet, cook chicken in oil over medium heat until a thermometer reads 170°, 6-8 minutes on each side. Meanwhile, in a small saucepan, melt butter. Stir in the flour, pepper, and salt until smooth. Gradually stir in the milk, broth, and sherry. Bring to a boil; cook and stir until thickened, 1-2 minutes. Stir in chives. Serve with chicken.

Nutrition: Calories: 274, Fat: 8g Cholesterol: 72mg, Sodium: 569mg,

Carbohydrate: 20g, Protein: 28g

39. Apple Cider BBQ Chicken Breast

Preparation Time: 20 minutes

Cooking Time: 3 ½ hours

Servings: 4

Ingredients: 1 tablespoon canola oil

4 bone-in chicken thighs (about 1-1/2 pounds), skin removed1/4 teaspoon salt

1/4 teaspoon pepper 2 medium Fuji or Gala apples, coarsely chopped

1 medium onion, chopped 1 garlic clove, minced 1/3 cup barbecue sauce

1/4 cup apple cider or juice 1 tablespoon honey

Directions:

In a large skillet, heat oil over medium heat. Brown chicken thighs on both sides; sprinkle with salt and pepper. Transfer to a 3-qt. slow cooker; top with apples.Add onion to same skillet; cook and stir over medium heat 2-3 minutes or until tender. Add garlic; cook 1 minute longer. Stir in barbecue sauce, apple cider and honey; increase heat to medium-high. Cook 1 minute, stirring to loosen browned bits from pan. Pour over chicken and apples. Cook, covered, on low 3-1/2 to 4-1/2 hours or until chicken is tender.Freeze option: Freeze cooled chicken mixture in freezer containers. To use, partially thaw in refrigerator overnight. Heat through in a covered saucepan, stirring occasionally.

Nutrition:

Calories: 333, Fat: 13g, Cholesterol: 87mg, Sodium: 456mg, Carbohydrate: 29g,

Protein: 25g

40. Green Chili Jack Chicken

Preparation Time: 5 minutes

Cooking Time: 20 minutes

Servings: 2 to 3

Ingredients:

1 lb. chicken strips 1 teaspoon chili powder 4 ounces green chilies

1 cup Monterey jack cheese ¼ cup salsa

Directions:

Spray a medium size frypan with cooking spray.

Sprinkle chili powder over chicken.

Cook chicken strips until no longer pink.

Turn stove top on low and add green chilis on top of chicken.

Cook until chilis are warmed.

Add cheese and cook until melted on top of chilis.

Put on a dish and serve with salsa on the side.

Nutrition:

Calories: 516, Total Fat 24.4 g, Saturated Fat 12.6 g,

Cholesterol 209 mg, Sodium 697.9 mg, Total Carbohydrate 8.5 g

Dietary Fiber 1.8 g, Sugars 4.3 g, Protein 64.2 g

41. Orange Chicken

Preparation Time: 10 minutes

Cooking Time: 40 minutes

Servings: 4

Ingredients: ¾ cup fresh squeezed orange juice

1 ½ teaspoon orange zest, grated ¾ cup chicken broth, reduced sodium

8 strips of orange peel (each approximately 2" long and ½" wide)

1 ½ pounds chicken thighs; skinless trimmed & cut in 1 ½" pieces

6 tablespoon distilled white vinegar ¼ cup soy sauce

8 small whole dried red chilies, optional ½ cup dark brown sugar, packed

1 tablespoon plus 2 teaspoon cornstarch 3 garlic cloves, pressed or minced

1-piece (1") ginger, grated 2 tablespoon cold water ¼ teaspoon cayenne pepper

For Coating & Frying:

1 cup cornstarch 3 large egg whites ¼ teaspoon cayenne pepper

3 cups peanut oil ½ teaspoon baking soda

Directions:

For the Marinade & Sauce:

Place the chicken thighs in a one-gallon zipper-lock bag; set aside. Now, combine the chicken broth together with grated zest, orange juice, ginger, soy sauce, vinegar, garlic, cayenne & sugar in large-sized saucepan; whisk until the sugar is completely dissolved.

Measure approximately ¾ cup of the prepared mixture out & pour into the bag with chicken; press out the air as much as possible & seal the bag; ensure that the pieces are coated well with the marinade. Refrigerate for 30 to 60 minutes. Bring the leftover mixture to a boil over high heat in the saucepan. Stir the cornstarch with cold water in a small bowl; whisk the cornstarch mixture into the sauce. Let the sauce to simmer for a minute, until thick & translucent, stirring occasionally. Turn off the heat and then stir in the orange peel & chilies; set the sauce aside.

For the Coating:

Place the egg whites in a pie plate; beat using a large fork until completely frothy. Whisk the cornstarch together with cayenne & baking soda in a second pie plate until combined well. Drain the chicken in a large mesh strainer or colander; thoroughly pat the chicken dry using paper towels. Place half of chicken pieces into the egg whites; turn to coat and then transfer the pieces to the cornstarch mixture; ensure that the pieces are thoroughly coated. Place the dredged chicken pieces on a wire rack set over the baking sheet; repeat with the leftover chicken pieces.

For the Chicken:

Now, over high heat in straight-sided sauté pan or 11 to 12" Dutch oven; heat up the oil until hot. Work in batches & carefully place half of the chicken into the oil one piece at a time; fry for a couple of minutes, until turn golden brown, turning each piece with tongs halfway during the cooking process. Transfer the chicken to a paper towels lined large plate. Heat up the oil & repeat the steps with the leftover chicken.

To Serve:

Reheat the sauce over medium heat for approximately 2 minutes, until simmering. Add in the chicken & toss gently until coated evenly & heated through. Serve immediately and enjoy.

Nutrition:

Calories: 490,

Total Fat: 23 g,

Cholesterol: 80 mg,

Sodium   : 820 mg,

Total Carbohydrate: 51 g,

Dietary Fiber: 2 g,

Sugars: 19 g,

Protein: 25 g

42. Fish Tacos

Preparation Time: 10 minutes

Cooking Time: 30 minutes

Servings: 4

Ingredients 1-pound halibut fillet, skin removed   ¼ green cabbage

10 corn tortillas, warmed   ¼ cup white onion, chopped

salsa

Juice of 1 lime, freshly squeezed   ¼ cup English cucumber, chopped

Guacamole

½ bunch of fresh cilantros, chopped   1 tablespoon olive oil Pepper & salt to taste

Directions:

For Cabbage Slaw:

In a large bowl add the chiffonade cabbage together with cucumber, onion & cilantro; squeeze the lime juice on top & toss well; sprinkle pepper & salt to taste; let sit for 30 minutes at room temperature. Preheat your oven to 400 F. Over medium heat in a non-stick oven proof pan; heat up the olive oil until hot and then carefully add the halibut; cook until the first side turn brown; turn over & put the pan in the preheated oven until the halibut is flakey & cooked through, for 10 to 15 minutes. Flake the cooked halibut into a bowl & serve with warmed corn tortillas & the bowls of the guacamole, cabbage slaw & salsa. Enjoy.

Nutrition: Calories: 230, Total Fat: 12 g,Cholesterol: 15 mg, Sodium: 470 mg

Total Carbohydrate: 26 g, Dietary Fiber: 3 g, Sugar: 2 g,   Protein:7g

Chapter 4 Desserts

43. Fried Apples Recipe

Preparation Time: 10 minutes

Cooking Time: 20 minutes

Servings: 8

Ingredients:

6 Granny Smith Apples - peeled and sliced (10 slices per apple) ¼ Cup of Margarine

¼ Cup Brown Sugar ⅛ Teaspoon Salt ⅛ Teaspoon of Nutmeg

1 Teaspoon of Cinnamon 1 Teaspoon of Lemon Juice

Directions:

Melt margarine in a large skillet over medium/low heat

Place apple slices in skillet - try and make it even. Pour lemon juice on top -- try and get the juice on as many apples as possible

Sprinkle brown sugar + Salt onto the apples.

Cover and cook for 15 minutes - turn over once

Make sure the apples are tender

Sprinkles Cinnamon and Nutmeg on Top of Apples

Nutrition:

Calories: 78,

Carbohydrates: 7g,

Protein: 0g,

Fat: 5g,

Saturated Fat: 3g,

Cholesterol: 15mg,

Sodium: 88mg,

Potassium: 9mg,

Fiber: 0g,

Sugar: 6g

44. Old Country Store Double Fudge Coca Cola Cake

Preparation Time: 10 minutes

Cooking Time: 30 minutes

Servings: 24

Ingredients: Cake 1 cup Coca-Cola 1/2 cup oil 1/2 cup or 1 stick margarine

3 tablespoons of cocoa 2 cups sugar 2 cups all-purpose flour 1/2 teaspoon salt

2 eggs 1/2 cup buttermilk 1 teaspoon baking soda 1 teaspoon vanilla

Frosting

1/2 cup or 1 stick of margarine 3 tablespoons cocoa 6 tablespoons cream or milk

1 teaspoon vanilla 1/2 to 1 cup chopped pecans 1-pound confectioners' sugar

Directions:

Cake

In a saucepan, bring Coca-Cola, oil, margarine, and cocoa to a boil. Mix the sugar, flour, and salt, pour into the boiling liquid, and beat well. Add the eggs, buttermilk, baking soda, and vanilla and beat well. Pour into a greased and floured sheet cake pan and bake at 350 degrees for 20-25 minutes.

Frosting

In a saucepan, combine the margarine, cocoa, and cream or milk and heat until the butter melts. Beat in the remaining ingredients. Spread on the hot cake. Cool and cut.

Nutrition: Calories: 334, Carbohydrates: 46g, Protein: 2g, Fat: 16g, Saturated Fat: 5g,

Cholesterol: 34mg, Sodium: 175mg, Potassium: 65mg, Fiber: 1g, Sugar: 36g

45. Chocolate Chip Pecan Pie

Preparation Time: 10 minutes

Cooking Time: 50 minutes

Servings: 8

Ingredients:3 eggs1/2 cup sugar1 cup corn syrup1/2 teaspoon salt

1 teaspoon vanilla extract1/4 cups melted margarine1 cups pecan

3 tablespoons semi-sweet chocolate chips

Plain pastry shell

Directions:

Preheat oven to 350 degrees. In a medium sized bowl, beat together eggs, and then add in sugar, mix well. Mix in corn syrup, salt, vanilla, and margarine. Place pecans and chocolate chips in pie shell. Add mixture. The pecans will rise up to the top when baking. Bake in a 350 degrees oven for 50-60 minutes.

You could serve this chocolate pecan pie with a scoop of vanilla ice cream.

Nutrition:

Calories: 460,Carbohydrates: 60g, Protein: 4g, Fat: 24g,

Saturated Fat: 7g, Cholesterol: 76mg,

Sodium: 333mg,Potassium: 126mg, Fiber: 2g,Sugar: 47g

46. Chocolate Cherry Cobbler

Preparation Time: 10 minutes

Cooking Time: 45 minutes

Servings: 8

Ingredients: 1 can (21 oz.) cherry pie filling 1½ cups flour ½ cup sugar

2 tsp baking powder ½ tsp salt ¼ cup (1/2 stick) cold butter 1 egg

1 cup (a 6 oz. bag) chocolate chips ¼ cup evaporated milk ½ cup slivered almonds

Directions:

Preheat oven to 350 degrees F. You will need a 1½ to 2-quart baking dish (I used a 1.5 QT oval).

Mix flour, sugar, salt & baking powder in a medium bowl. Cut butter into chunks and add to the flour mixture.

Cut in butter until the mixture resembles small peas. Set aside. Spread cherry pie filling in the bottom of a 1.5 to 2-quart baking dish. Set aside. Melt chocolate chips either in the microwave or stovetop. Stir frequently until the chips are all melted, and mixture is smooth. Cool for about 5 minutes. Add evaporated milk and egg to melted chocolate chips. Stir until well blended. Add the chocolate mixture to the flour mixture. Mix very well. Drop randomly on top of cherry filling in baking dish. Sprinkle with the almonds. Bake at 350 degrees F for 40-45 minutes. Serve warm with ice cream, whipped cream, or cream.

Nutrition: Calories: 460, Carbohydrates: 65g, Protein: 6g, Fat: 19g,

Saturated Fat: 9g, Cholesterol: 37mg, Sodium: 225mg, Potassium: 396mg, Fiber: 3g,

Sugar: 20g

47. Apple Dumpling Bake

Preparation Time: 15 minutes

Cooking Time: 35 minutes

Servings: 8

Ingredients:

2 medium Granny Smith apples 2 tubes (8 ounces each) refrigerated crescent rolls

1 cup sugar 1/3 cup butter, softened 1/2 teaspoon ground cinnamon

3/4 cup Mountain Dew soda

Vanilla ice cream

Directions:

Preheat oven to 350°. Peel, core and cut each apple into 8 wedges. Unroll both tubes of crescent dough; separate each into 8 triangles. Wrap a triangle around each wedge. Place in a greased 13x9-in. baking dish.

In a bowl, mix sugar, butter, and cinnamon until blended, sprinkle over dumplings. Slowly pour soda around the rolls (do not stir).

Bake, uncovered, until golden brown and apples are tender, 35-40 minutes. Serve warm with ice cream.

Nutrition:

Calories: 414, Fat: 20g, Saturated fat: 9g, Cholesterol: 20mg, Sodium: 510mg,

Carbohydrate: 510mg, Sugar: 510mg, Fiber: 1g, Protein: 4g

48. Homemade Corn Muffins with Honey Butter

Preparation Time: 20 minutes

Cooking Time: 20 minutes

Servings: 16

Ingredients:

1/4 cup butter, softened 1/4 cup reduced-fat cream cheese 1/2 cup sugar 2 large eggs

1-1/2 cups fat-free milk 1-1/2 cups all-purpose flour 1-1/2 cups yellow cornmeal

4 teaspoons baking powder 3/4 teaspoon salt

Honey Butter:

1/4 cup butter, softened 2 tablespoons honey

Directions:

In a large bowl, cream the butter, cream cheese, and sugar until light and fluffy.

Add eggs, one at a time, beating well after each addition.

Stir in the milk. Combine the flour, cornmeal, baking powder and salt; add to creamed mixture just until moistened. Coat muffin cups with cooking spray; fill three-fourths full of batter. Bake at 400° for 18-22 minutes or until a toothpick inserted in the center comes out clean. Cool for 5 minutes before removing from pans to wire racks.

Beat butter and honey until blended; serve with warm muffins.

Nutrition: Calories: 198, Fat: 7g, Cholesterol: 45mg, Sodium: 285mg,

Carbohydrate: 29g, Protein: 4g

49. Peach Cobbler with Almond Crumble Topping

Preparation Time: 15 minutes

Cooking Time: 1 hour

Servings: 6 to 9

Ingredients:

BATTER

1 cup cracker barrel pancake mix (can substitute but I would not) 1 cup milk

½ cup melted butter ¼ teaspoon nutmeg ½ teaspoon cinnamon

FILLING

2 (15 ounce) cans peach slices in heavy syrup or (15 ounce) cans diced peaches in heavy syrup

¼ cup sugar

TOPPING

½ cup brown sugar 1/8 cup flour ½ teaspoon cinnamon 1 tablespoon softened butter

sliced almonds

Directions:

Mix all batter ingredients in a bowl with whisk until well incorporated and light. Pour into non greased 8 x 8 baking pan.

Drain peaches of syrup except for about a tablespoon of juice in each can and mix with sugar until it has dissolved. Pour over batter but do not mix -- batter will rise over peaches and juices on its own.

Mix all topping ingredients with hands slightly breaking up almonds as you incorporate. Do not place on cobbler yet as the almonds will burn! That step will come later.

Place into 375-degree oven for 45 minutes. Then, while leaving cobbler in oven, place crumble topping over cobbler and bake another 10-15 minutes. Watch carefully so that nuts do not burn.

Serve while still a little warm with some cinnamon ice cream and enjoy!

Nutrition:

Calories: 475.1,

Total Fat: 20.1 g.

Cholesterol: 56 mg,

Sodium 449 mg,

Total Carbohydrate 72.2 g,

Dietary Fiber 2.6 g,

Sugars 46.9 g,

Protein 4.8 g

50. Banana Pudding

Preparation Time: 10 minutes

Cooking Time: 30 minutes

Servings: 6

Ingredients:

Pudding

3/4 cup sugar

1/3 cup all-purpose flour

3 cups whole milk

4 beaten egg yolks

3 tablespoons butter

2 ounces cream cheese

2 teaspoons vanilla

Banana Pudding

48 vanilla wafers

1 cup heavy whipping cream whipped

1 teaspoon sugar

2 large bananas

Directions:

Pudding

In a heavy saucepan combine sugar, flour, and milk. Cook and stir continually over medium heat until the mixture is thickened and bubbly. Cook and stir for an additional two minutes. Remove from heat.

Place for egg yolks in a small bowl. Beat eggs well. Place 1 cup of the hot pudding mixture slowly into the beaten eggs. Stir the egg mixture well, and then slowly add this into the pan where the remainder of the pudding is. Cook the mixture until it just begins to bubble. Add butter, cream cheese, and vanilla. Stir until all of the ingredients are well incorporated.

Pour the pudding into a bowl. Place plastic wrap on the surface of the pudding. Place pudding into the refrigerator to cool.

Whipped Cream

Place 1 cup of heavy whipping cream into a bowl with 1 teaspoon of sugar.

Using either a whisk or a mixer, beat the whipping cream until it becomes stiff. Refrigerate, and use immediately.

Assembling the pudding

Break for vanilla wafers into each jar, cut bananas into slices, place 4 or 5 slices of bananas into each jar. Add a couple of tablespoons of pudding on top of the bananas. Repeat 2 more times in each jar. Top with whipped cream.

Nutrition:

Calories: 723, Carbohydrates: 84g, Protein: 10g, Fat: 39g,

Saturated Fat: 21g, Cholesterol: 223mg, Sodium: 348mg, Potassium: 427mg,

Fiber: 2g, Sugar: 53g

51. Campfire S'more

Preparation Time: 15 minutes

Cooking Time: 40 minutes

Servings: 9

Ingredients:

Graham Cracker Crust

2 cups graham cracker crumbs

1/4 cup sugar 1/2 cup butter 1/2 teaspoon cinnamon

1 small package of brownie mix enough for an 8 x 8 pan or use the brownie ingredients listed below.

Brownie Mix

1/2 cup flour 1/3 cup cocoa (Hershey's) 1/4 teaspoon baking powder

1/4 teaspoon salt 1/2 cup butter 1 cup sugar 1 teaspoon vanilla 2 large eggs

Smore's Topping

9 marshmallows 5 Hershey candy bars 4 1/2 cups vanilla ice cream

1/2 cup chocolate sauce

Directions:

Preheat the oven to 350 degrees. Make the graham cracker crust by mixing together the graham cracker crumbs, sugar, cinnamon, and melted butter in a large bowl. Stir until well combined. Line an 8 x 8-inch baking pan with waxed paper or parchment paper. Make sure the paper is larger than the pan, you will later lift the brownies out of the pan when they are done. Press the graham cracker crumbs into the pan.

Place the pan into the oven while you are making the brownies. Prepare the brownies by sifting together flour, cocoa, baking powder, and salt. Melt butter in a 10 - 12 cup saucepan over moderate heat. Stir in sugar and vanilla and add eggs one at a time. Stir in dry ingredients and stir in nuts. Spread smoothly over the graham cracker crust. Cook the brownies for 23 to 25 minutes. Allow the brownies to cool in the pan.

When the brownies have cooled completely, gently lift them out of the pan. Cut the brownies into 9 equal portions. When you are ready to serve the brownies, top each one with a large marshmallow and place the brownie under the broiler in your oven. Cook for a few moments until the marshmallow begins to brown. When the marshmallow has browned remove it from the oven, and then top with 1/2 of a Hershey bar. Serve with vanilla ice cream and top the vanilla ice cream with chocolate sauce.

Nutrition:

Calories: 888,

Carbohydrates: 125g, Protein: 10g,

Fat: 39g, Saturated Fat: 20g,

Cholesterol: 124mg, Sodium: 667mg,

Potassium: 298mg, Fiber: 2g, Sugar: 84g

52. Strawberry Shortcake

Preparation Time: 10 minutes

Cooking Time: 10 minutes

Servings: 8

Ingredients: Quick and Easy

1 pre-made pound cake 1-pint frozen sweetened strawberries

4 scoops premium vanilla ice cream 1 can whipped cream

Scratch Method 4 scoops vanilla ice cream

1 homemade pound cake 1-pound Fresh strawberries 1-pint whipped cream

Directions:Quick and Easy Assembly Assemble strawberry shortcake by cutting two slices of the pound cake and then slicing those in half. † In a bowl, place the 4 pieces of pound cake across from each other. Spoon defrosted strawberries onto cake; add one scoop of vanilla ice cream and top with whipped cream. While the Cracker Barrel may use frozen strawberries, I really like fresh much more. I think you can jazz up this recipe by using fresh strawberries, fresh whipped cream, and if you are up for it, a homemade pound cake. From Scratch Method Prepare the strawberries several hours ahead of time by cleaning them, slicing them, and placing them into a bowl. Add about 1 tablespoon of superfine sugar, if available, to the strawberries and mix well. Place strawberries in the refrigerator. The sugar will help to make the strawberries juicy. Whip the whipping cream with a mixer until firm. You may want to add a touch of vanilla to this for some extra flavor. When you are ready to serve the shortcakes, follow the directions above.

Nutrition: Calories: 542, Carbohydrates: 77g, Protein: 9g, Fat: 22g, Saturated Fat: 13g, Cholesterol: 150mg, Sodium: 460mg, Potassium: 469mg, Fiber: 3g, Sugar: 51g

53. Pumpkin Custard N' Ginger Snaps

Preparation Time: 30 minutes

Cooking Time: 35 minutes

Servings: 8

Ingredients: 8 egg yolks

1 3/4 cup pure pumpkin puree - 1 (15 ounce) can of pure pumpkin

1 3/4 cup heavy whipping cream 1/2 cup granulated sugar

1 1/2 teaspoon pumpkin pie spice 1 teaspoon vanilla

1 cup ginger snap cookies and about 8 ginger snap cookies that are whole

1 tablespoon melted butter 1 cup heavy whipping cream

1 tablespoon granulated sugar if you have extra fine sugar this is best

1/2 teaspoon pumpkin pie spice

Directions:

Preheat oven to 350 degrees.

Crack open 8 eggs and separate the whites from the yolks. In a medium-sized glass bowl add egg yolks and whisk until they are creamy. Add pumpkin, 1/2 cup sugar, vanilla, 1 3/4 cups of heavy cream, and pumpkin pie spice and combine until all are incorporated.

Cook custard mixture in a double boiler, and stir until custard has thickened, and a spoon remains coated when inserted into the custard. Pour custard into either 8 custard dishes, or an 8 x 8 baking dish. Bake custard for about 30-35 minutes or until a spoon is inserted comes out clean.

Halfway through the baking process combine the 1 cup gingersnaps and 1 tablespoon melted butter, and sprinkle the crumb mixture over the custard while it is baking by removing the dishes from the oven, adding gingersnap crumb mixture and returning the dishes to the oven to finish baking. If you are using small individual custard dishes check the custard at 20-25 minutes. Allow the custard to cool to room temperature.

Just before serving mix the pumpkin pie spice-infused whipped cream by whisking together the 1 cup whipping cream, 1 tablespoon granulated sugar, and 1/4 teaspoon pumpkin pie spice until the whipped cream is thickened.

Nutrition:

Calories: 487,

Carbohydrates: 32g,

Protein: 5g,

Fat: 38g,

Saturated Fat: 21g,

Cholesterol: 311mg,

Sodium: 126mg,

Potassium: 240mg,

Fiber: 1g,

Sugar: 18g

54. Old Country Store Carrot Cake

Preparation Time: 20 minutes

Cooking Time: 50 minutes

Servings: 24

Ingredients:

Cake ingredients

3/4 cup finely chopped English walnuts 2 cups finely shredded carrots

8 ounces crushed pineapple do not drain 1/2 cup finely shredded coconut

1/2 cup raisins that have been soaked in water until plump and then drained

1 1/4 cup vegetable oil 1 1/2 cup sugar 1/2 cup brown sugar

3 eggs

3 cups all-purpose flour

2 teaspoons baking powder

2 teaspoons baking soda

2 teaspoons vanilla

2 teaspoons ground cinnamon

1 teaspoon ground nutmeg

1/2 teaspoon ground cloves

1/2 teaspoon salt

Cream Cheese Frosting

8 ounces cream cheese

4 ounces butter at room temperature 1 teaspoon vanilla 2 cups powdered sugar

1/2 cup chopped pecans for garnish

Directions:

For the Cake

Mix together flour, baking powder, baking soda, salt, cinnamon, nutmeg, and cloves. Set aside. In a large bowl, mix the vegetable oil, sugars, vanilla, and eggs until smooth and fluffy. Add pineapple, walnuts, coconut, carrots, and raisins and blend well. Gradually add flour mixture a half at a time until blended through.

Pour batter into a greased and floured 9x13 inch pan and bake at 350 degrees for about 40-50 minutes. Test with a toothpick for doneness. When cool, frost with cream cheese frosting.

For the Cream Cheese Frosting

Blend cream cheese and butter until light and fluffy. Add vanilla and a little of the powdered sugar at a time until all has been blended well. Turn mixer on high and beat until frosting is light and fluffy. Spread frosting over the cooled cake and sprinkle with pecans.

Nutrition:

Calories: 318, Carbohydrates: 45g, Protein: 4g,

Fat: 14g, Saturated Fat: 6g, Cholesterol: 41mg, Sodium: 222mg,

Potassium: 182mg, Fiber: 1g, Sugar: 29g

55. Cinnabon Cinnamon Swirl Cheesecake

Preparation Time: 25 minutes

Cooking Time: 1 hour & 40 minutes

Servings: 8

Ingredients

17 rectangles graham crackers 1 tablespoon butter flavoring

3 tablespoons cornstarch 1 ⅓ cups raw sugar 5 tablespoon vegan margarine, melted

⅔ cup vegan sour cream

3 packages of vegan cream cheese, at room temperature (8 ounce)

1 teaspoon lemon zest 2 tablespoon vanilla nut & butter flavoring

1 tablespoon almond milk 3 tablespoon raw sugar

½ cup firm tofu 2 teaspoon cinnamon ½ cup dark brown sugar

reserved 3/8 cup of the batter

Directions:

Generously grease the bottom & sides of a spring form pan then line the bottom with wax paper and preheat your oven to 350 F.

Form the crust by melting the margarine; add in the butter flavoring, mix well & set aside.

Now, grind the graham crackers in a food processor and then add in the sugar, process for on high speed for a minute.

Combine the butter mixtures together with graham cracker in a medium bowl until incorporated well. Press the mixture to the bottom of the spring form pan; set aside.

Prepare the batter by blending ⅓ cup of the sugar and cornstarch with a package of the cream cheese for a couple of minutes on low. Stop; scrape down the sides of your bowl and then slowly add in the leftover cream cheese; do not forget to scrape the sides of your bowl down, as required.

Combine the leftover sugar with lemon zest. Increase the speed to medium & add lemon sugar into the cream cheese mixture. Add in the vanilla; scrape the sides & set aside.

Combine tofu with almond milk in a blender or food processor until completely smooth. Mix in tofu mixture into the batter on medium speed. Add in the sour cream; mix well & scrape the sides again.

Reserve approximately 3/8 cup of the batter for swirl mixture. Pour the leftover batter into the prepared pan over the crust; set aside.

For swirl mixture take the kept-aside batter together with cinnamon & brown sugar; combine well. Scoop a few tablespoons full of the cinnamon mixture over the cheesecake; pressing it down gently with a spoon. Swirl the cinnamon using a knife tip to.

Bake in the preheated oven for 60 to 75 minutes. Let cool for a few hours. Cover & let refrigerate for 4 hours more. Garnish with the brown rice syrup and chopped pecans; serve immediately & enjoy.

Nutrition: Calories: 1370, Total Fat: 85g, Cholesterol: 275mg, Sodium: 710mg,

Total Carbohydrate: 141g, Dietary Fiber: 2g, Sugars: 120g, Protein: 10g

56. Peanut Butter Cheesecake

Preparation Time: 8 hours & 15 minutes

Cooking Time: 2 hours & 5 minutes

Servings: 16

Ingredients:

For Chocolate Cake:

1 ¾ cup all-purpose flour 1 cup buttermilk 2 teaspoon baking soda

Heaping ¾ cup of cocoa

2 cup sugar 1 tablespoon vanilla extract

2 eggs room temp 1 cup black coffee hot ½ cup butter melted 1 teaspoon salt

For Cheesecake:

12 fun-sized Reese's Peanut Butter cups; chopped

1 ¼ cup sugar 4 packages full-fat cream cheese (8ounces each), softened

½ cup sour cream

5 large eggs, organic 1 can of dulce de leche (14ounces) 2 teaspoon vanilla extract

For Peanut Butter Buttercream:

4-5 cups powdered sugar 1 ½ teaspoon vanilla

¾ cup each of butter, peanut butter & shortening

For Ganache:

1 cup heavy cream 2 cups semi-sweet chocolate chips 1 teaspoon vanilla

Directions:

For the Chocolate Cake:

Line the bottoms of 2 round baking pans, 9" each with the parchment paper; coat it lightly with the cooking spray; set aside and then preheat your oven to 350 F in advance. Combine the flour together with baking soda, cocoa, sugar & salt in a large bowl; mix well. Slowly add in the eggs followed by the butter, buttermilk & vanilla; continue to mix after each addition until completely smooth. Fold in the hot coffee and mix until a runny batter form. Pour the prepared batter into the baking pans & bake in the preheated oven for 30 to 35 minutes. Remove from the oven & let cool in the pans for approximately 10 minutes then invert them onto the cooling racks. Once completely cool, wrap in the saran wrap & refrigerate.

For the Cheesecake:

Preheat your oven to 475 F. Fill large pan with approximately ½" of water & lightly coat a standard-sized spring-form pan, 9" with the non-stick cooking spray; wrap the bottom in a tinfoil. Combine the cream cheese using an electric mixer in a large bowl until completely fluffy. Add in the sugar, vanilla, and sour cream; continue to mix until combined well. Slowly mix in the eggs (ensure that you blend well after every addition) and then fold in the chopped Reese's Peanut Butter Cups.

Pour into your prepared pan & place the pan in water dish. Bake in the preheated oven for 10 minutes; decrease the heat settings to 350 & continue baking until the cheesecake is just set, for 50 to 60 more minutes. Remove from the oven & let cool. Once done; cover & let refrigerate for overnight. Once cooled; trim off approximately ½ to 1" of the tops of the cheesecake to make level & then split the cake in half using a serrated knife or cake leveler. Let chill in a refrigerator until ready for use. Now prepare the peanut butter-butter cream by creaming the butter together with shortening; once fluffy, immediately add in the vanilla & peanut butter. Adding one cup at a time; add in the powdered sugar and continue to cream until you get your desired level of consistency; set aside. Add dulce de leche to a large bowl & add some teaspoons of the milk to thin out.

To Assemble:

Add 1 of your layers of chocolate cake either on a cake or turntable stand & top with half of the dulce de leche. Top the dulce de leche with a layer of cheesecake. Spread with approximately a cup of the peanut butter-butter cream & top with a layer more of cheesecake. Spread the leftover dulce de leche & top with a layer of cake as well. Trip the outside of cake, if required and make it even & spread a thin layer of your peanut butter-butter cream to do a crumb coating and seal any spaces or gaps in the cake. Place in the freezer until slightly harden up, for half an hour. In the meantime, prepare the ganache. Add the chocolate chips to heat proof bowl & add in the heavy cream to the saucepan; heat until it just begins to boil, over moderate heat. Pour the cream on top of the chocolate chips; cover for 5 to 7 minutes. Remove the cover & stir until the chocolate completely melted into the cream. Let sit until slightly thickens. Remove the cake from freeze & pour some of the ganache on top and spread down the sides of your cake. Repeat until sides and top of cake are completely covered. Place ¼ cup of the peanut butter in small bowl & heat for a couple of minutes (over medium-low heat), until liquid then drizzle on top of the cake. Carefully decorate the bottom and top of your cake with the leftover buttercream.

Nutrition:

Calories: 592, Total Fat: 42g Cholesterol: 138mg, Sodium: 436mg, Potassium: 270mg,

Total Carbohydrates: 45g, Dietary Fiber: 1.5g, Sugar: 32g, Protein: 12g

Chapter 5 Beef and Pork

57. Beef Stew

Preparation Time: 10 minutes

Cooking Time: 2 hours

Servings: 8

Ingredients:

1-pound stewing beef, in medium sized chunks 3 tablespoons vegetable oil, divided

Salt and pepper, to taste 1/2 cup flour1 onion, chopped

4 medium potatoes, cut into chunks

5 carrots, peeled and cut into chunks 1-quart beef broth 1/3 cup ketchup

1 cup peas

Directions:

Mix the flour with salt and pepper to taste and toss with the meat.

Add 2 tablespoons of oil to a large pot and over medium high heat brown beef in flour, add all the flour.

Stir often so the flour and meat, do not burn, but brown nicely. Remove meat to a plate.

Add the last tablespoon of oil and sauté the onion until translucent scraping up a browned bit from the meat.

Transfer the meat back to the pot, add the potatoes and carrots. Add the stock and ketchup. Stir well to combine.

Simmer over low heat, stirring often for 1 1/2 hours. Adjust seasoning.

Add frozen peas just before serving. Stir to defrost and serve.

Nutrition:

Calories: 178, Carbohydrates: 17g, Protein: 16g, Fat: 4g, Saturated Fat: 2g,

Cholesterol: 35mg, Sodium: 209mg, Potassium: 602mg, Fiber: 3g, Sugar: 3g

58. Meat Loaf

Preparation Time: 15 minutes

Cooking Time: 1 ½ hours

Servings: 6

Ingredients: 2 large eggs 2/3 cup whole milk 3 slices bread, torn

1/2 cup chopped onion 1/2 cup grated carrot

1 cup shredded cheddar or part-skim mozzarella cheese

1 tablespoon minced fresh parsley or 1 teaspoon dried parsley

1 teaspoon dried basil, thyme, or sage, optional 1 teaspoon salt 1/4 teaspoon pepper

1-1/2 pounds lean ground beef

TOPPING:

1/2 cup tomato sauce 1/2 cup packed brown sugar 1 teaspoon prepared mustard

Directions:

In a large bowl, beat eggs. Add milk and bread; let stand until liquid is absorbed. Stir in the onion, carrot, cheese, and seasonings. Crumble beef over mixture and mix well. Shape into a 7-1/2x3-1/2x2-1/2-in. loaf in a shallow baking pan. Bake, uncovered, at 350° for 45 minutes. Combine the topping ingredients, spoon half of the mixture over meat loaf. Bake 30 minutes longer or until meat is no longer pink and a thermometer reads 160°, occasionally spooning remaining topping over loaf. Let stand 10 minutes before serving.

Nutrition: Calories: 398, Fat: 17g, Saturated fat: 9g, Cholesterol: 164mg,

Sodium: 771mg, Carbohydrate: 29g, Sugar: 22g, Fiber: 1g, Protein: 30g

59. Roast Beef

Preparation Time: 20 minutes

Cooking Time: 2 ½ hours

Servings: 8

Ingredients: 1 tablespoon canola oil 1 beef eye round roast (about 2-1/2 pounds)

1 garlic clove, minced 2 teaspoons dried basil 1 teaspoon salt

1 teaspoon dried rosemary, crushed 1/2 teaspoon pepper 1 medium onion, chopped

1 teaspoon beef bouillon granules 1 cup brewed coffee 3/4 cup water

Gravy:

1/4 cup all-purpose flour 1/4 cup cold water

Directions:

In a Dutch oven, heat oil over medium heat; brown roast on all sides. Remove from pan. Mix garlic and seasonings, sprinkle over roast.

Add onion to same pan; cook and stir over medium heat until tender; stir in bouillon, coffee and 3/4 cup water. Add roast; bring to a boil. Reduce heat; simmer, covered, until meat is tender, about 2-1/2 hours. Remove roast from pan, reserving cooking juices. Tent with foil; let stand 10 minutes before slicing. Mix flour and cold water until smooth; stir into cooking juices. Bring to a boil, stirring constantly. Cook and stir until thickened, 1-2 minutes. Serve with roast.

Nutrition: Calories: 198, Fat: 6g, Cholesterol: 65mg, Sodium: 453mg,

Carbohydrate: 5g, Protein: 28g

60. Grilled Pork Chops

Preparation Time: 20 minutes

Cooking Time: 10 minutes

Servings: 4

Ingredients: 1/4 cup kosher salt 1/4 cup sugar 2 cups water

2 cups ice water 4 center-cut pork rib chops (1 inch thick and 8 ounces each)

2 tablespoons canola oil

Basic Rub:

3 tablespoons paprika

1 teaspoon each garlic powder, onion powder, ground cumin and ground mustard

1 teaspoon coarsely ground pepper 1/2 teaspoon ground chipotle pepper

Directions: In a large saucepan, combine salt, sugar and 2 cups water; cook and stir over medium heat until salt and sugar are dissolved. Remove from heat. Add 2 cups ice water to cool brine to room temperature. Place pork chops in a large resealable plastic bag; add cooled brine. Seal bag, pressing out as much air as possible; turn to coat chops. Place in a 13x9-in. baking dish. Refrigerate 8-12 hours. Remove chops from brine, rinse, and pat dry. Discard brine. Brush both sides of chops with oil. In a small bowl, mix rub ingredients; rub over pork chops. Let stand at room temperature 30 minutes. Grill chops on an oiled rack, covered, over medium heat 4-6 minutes on each side or until a thermometer reads 145°. Let stand 5 minutes before serving.

Nutrition: Calories: 300, Fat: 18g, Cholesterol: 72mg, Sodium: 130mg,

Carbohydrate: 5g, Protein: 30g

61. Peppered Ribeye Steaks

Preparation Time: 10 minutes

Cooking Time: 10 minutes

Servings: 8

Ingredients: 1 tablespoon garlic powder 1 tablespoon paprika

2 teaspoons dried ground thyme 2 teaspoons dried ground oregano

1-1/2 teaspoons kosher salt 1-1/2 teaspoons pepper

1 teaspoon lemon-pepper seasoning 1 teaspoon cayenne pepper

1 teaspoon crushed red pepper flakes

4 beef ribeye steaks (1-1/2 inches thick and 8 ounces each)

Directions:

Combine all seasonings. Sprinkle over steaks, pressing mixture into both sides to help it adhere. Refrigerate, covered, for at least 1 hour or up to 24 hours. Remove steaks; blot with paper towels to remove any surface moisture, taking care to leave as much garlic mixture on steaks as possible. If desired, sprinkle with additional kosher salt. Grill steaks, covered, turning occasionally, on a greased grill rack over medium indirect heat until a thermometer reads 110°. Move steaks to direct heat; continue grilling until meat reaches desired doneness (for medium-rare, a thermometer should read 135°; medium, 140°; medium-well, 145°). Let stand 5 minutes before slicing. Place on a warm serving platter; cut across grain into thick slices.

Nutrition: Calories: 257, Fat: 18g, Cholesterol: 67mg, Sodium: 453mg,

Carbohydrate: 2g, Protein: 21g

62. Mushroom Braised Pot Roast

Preparation Time: 10 minutes

Cooking Time: 1 hour 30 minutes

Servings: 10

Ingredients: 4 pounds chuck roast 2 tablespoons vegetable oil 1/2 teaspoon salt

1/4 teaspoon pepper 1 cup chopped onion 2 cups beef broth

2 tablespoons gravy master 2 tablespoons butter

1-pound cremini mushrooms sliced or white button mushrooms

1/2 teaspoon salt

Directions:

Season roast with salt and pepper. Add vegetable oil to the Instant Pot. Sear roast on all sides until brown. Add 1 chopped onion to the Instant Pot along with 2 cups of beef broth, and 2 tablespoons of Gravy Master. Use the meat-setting button for 90 minutes.

Allow the pot to release by using the natural release method.

While the pot is releasing the pressure, naturally sauté 1 pound of sliced mushrooms butter.

Add 1/2 teaspoon of salt to the mushrooms while sautéing.

When mushrooms are cooked through, add to the roast.

Nutrition: Calories: 392, Carbohydrates: 3g, Protein: 37g, Fat: 26g,

Saturated Fat: 12g, Cholesterol: 131mg, Sodium: 782mg, Potassium: 862mg,

Fiber: 0g, Sugar: 1g

63. Shepherd's Pie

Preparation time: 10 minutes

Cooking time: 20 minutes

Servings: 4

Ingredients: 1-pound ground beef 1 cup onion, diced 2 cups frozen corn, thawed

2 cups frozen peas, thawed 2 tablespoons ketchup 1 tablespoon Worcestershire sauce

2 teaspoons garlic, minced 1 tablespoon cornstarch 1 teaspoon beef bouillon granules

½ cup cold water ½ cup sour cream

3 ½ cups mashed potatoes (prepared with milk and butter)

¾ cup shredded cheddar cheese

Directions

In a large skillet, brown the ground beef and onion over medium-high heat. Drain off any excess fat. Add the corn, peas, ketchup, Worcestershire sauce, and garlic. Stir well to combine, and then reduce the heat to medium low and cook for approximately 5 minutes, or until mixture the becomes bubbly. Make a slurry by stirring the corn starch and bouillon into the ½ cup of water. Stir until it is smooth, then stir it into the beef mixture and cook for about 2 more minutes. Stir in the sour cream and heat through. Cover the mixture with the mashed potatoes, and sprinkle on the cheese. Place the lid on the skillet and cook until the cheese melts. Serve.

Nutrition: Calories: 693 Total Fat: 40g, Saturated Fat: 17g, Cholesterol: 174mg,

Sodium: 1481mg, Potassium: 1499mg, Carbohydrates: 52g

64. Steak Diane

Preparation time: 10 minutes

Cooking time: 15 minutes

Servings: 2

Ingredients: 2–3 tablespoons butter

12 ounces beef tenderloin, cut into 3-ounce medallions Salt to taste

2 teaspoons cracked whole black peppercorns ½ cup fresh mushrooms, sliced

3 tablespoons pearl onions, chopped ¼ cup brandy or white wine

1 teaspoon Worcestershire sauce 1 tablespoon Dijon mustard ¾ cup beef stock

¼ cup cream

Directions:

Preheat the oven to 350°F. In a large skillet, melt 2 tablespoons of the butter over medium-high heat. Sprinkle both sides of the beef medallions with salt and fresh pepper. Sear them for about 2 minutes on each side, and then remove them from the skillet to an ovenproof dish and transfer it to the oven to keep warm. While those are in the oven, add a bit more butter to the skillet. Add the mushrooms and pearl onions and cook until they start to turn soft. Add the white wine and Worcestershire, then stir in the mustard. Cook for about 2 minutes. Stir in the beef stock and bring it to a boil. When it boils, remove it from the heat and stir in the cream. Remove the beef from the oven and plate it with sauce over the top.

Nutrition: Calories: 328.7, Total Fat: 21.7 g, Cholesterol: 78.9 mg, Sodium : 312.5 mg, Potassium: 403.9 mg, Carbohydrate: 4.5 g, Sugars:1.1 g, Protein: 22.5 g

65. Pasta Carbonara

Preparation time: 5 minutes

Cooking time: 20 minutes

Servings: 4

Ingredients: 4 slices bacon 2 tablespoons butter 2 cloves garlic, minced

2 tablespoons all-purpose flour ¼ cup Parmesan cheese, grated, plus more for serving

1 (12-ounce) can low-fat evaporated milk 1 cup frozen peas, thawed

8 ounces spaghetti, cooked ½ –1 cup hot chicken broth or pasta water, as needed

Salt and coarsely ground black pepper to taste

2 tablespoons fresh Italian parsley, snipped

Directions:

In a medium skillet, cook the bacon until it is crispy. Let it cool, and then break it into bite-sized pieces. In a large saucepan, melt the butter and add the garlic. Cook until it is fragrant and whisk in the flour and Parmesan cheese. Cook about 2 minutes.

Next, a little at a time, whisk in the evaporated milk. Bring this to a boil, then reduce the heat and cook until it thickens. Stir in the peas.

Put the cooked spaghetti in a large bowl and add half a cup of either chicken broth or pasta water, and then stir in the sauce. If the sauce is too thick you can thin it with more water or broth. Stir in the bacon pieces and serve with grated Parmesan and salt and pepper to taste. Sprinkle with parsley.

Nutrition: Calories: 1018, Total Fat: 33g, Cholesterol: 186mg, Sodium: 965mg,

Potassium: 386mg, Total Carbohydrates: 133g, Sugars: 2.5g Protein 44g

66. Grilled Steak Medallions

Preparation time: 10 minutes

Cooking time: 35 minutes

Servings: 8

Ingredients: 1-pound sirloin steak, cut into medallions or individual pieces

Salt and pepper to taste 1 tablespoon extra-virgin olive oil

3 tablespoons unsalted butter 3 cups mushrooms, sliced

1 medium-large shallot, minced 1 tablespoon garlic, minced

10 asparagus spears, chopped at an angle 1 cup grape tomatoes, halved

2 tablespoons flour ½ cup red wine ½ cup low-sodium beef broth

¼ teaspoon dried thyme, or one sprig of fresh thyme 1 bay leaf

Directions: Season the meat with salt and pepper. In a large skillet, heat the olive oil until it is hot. Add the steaks and cook for 4 minutes on the first side without moving them. After 4 minutes, flip and cook an additional 2 minutes. Remove the steaks from the skillet and cover with foil to keep them warm. Add 3 tablespoons of butter to the skillet. After it melts, add the mushrooms, shallots, garlic, and asparagus. Let them cook for 2–3 minutes, then stir and continue cooking until the asparagus starts to get soft. Add the grape tomatoes to heat them through. Add the flour and stir to combine, and then whisk in the red wine, beef broth, thyme, and bay leaf. Bring to a boil and cook until it starts to thicken. Remove the bay leaf before serving. Serve steak medallions with sauce and vegetables on top.

Nutrition: Calories: 440, Total Fat: 19g, Cholesterol: 140mg, Sodium: 1320mg,

Carbohydrates: 24g, Dietary Fiber: 4g, Sugars: 6g, Protein: 45g

67. Provolone Stuffed Meatballs

Preparation time: 15 minutes

Cooking time: 25 minutes

Servings: 4

Ingredients:

½ pound ground beef ½ pound ground veal 1-pound ground pork

½ cup breadcrumbs 2 tablespoons fresh parsley (minced) 1 egg (slightly beaten)

⅓ cup milk 3 cloves garlic, minced 1 teaspoon salt

½ teaspoon ground black pepper 3 ounces provolone cheese, cut into cubes

2 tablespoons olive oil 2 cups marinara sauce 2 cups alfredo sauce

1-pound fettuccine pasta

¼ cup chopped fresh parsley for serving

½ cup Parmesan cheese, grated, for serving

Directions:

In a large bowl, mix together the beef, veal, pork, breadcrumbs, parsley, egg, milk, garlic, salt, and pepper. Mix with your hands to make sure it is completely blended. Form into meatballs, but do not overwork the meat or your meatballs will be tough. Press your thumb into the balls as you form them and place a cube of the cheese inside. Reform the meatball around it.

In a heavy skillet, heat 2 teaspoons of olive oil over medium-high heat. When the oil is hot, add the meatballs, and brown them on all sides. When they are browned, transfer the balls to a plate line with paper towels to drain. (They will finish cooking in the sauce.)

Transfer the meatballs to a medium-sized saucepan and add the marinara sauce. Cook over medium to low heat for about 25 minutes.

Cook your fettuccine in a pot of boiling water until al dente, drain, and return to the pot. Add the Alfredo sauce. Heat and stir until the Alfredo sauce is hot.

To serve, place a bed of the fettuccine with Alfredo sauce on a serving plate, and scoop on some meatballs with a bit of marinara over the top. Sprinkle with fresh parsley and Parmesan.

Nutrition:

Calories: 1550,

Total Fat: 97g,

Saturated Fat: 46g,

Trans Fat: 2.5g,

Cholesterol 0mg,

Sodium: 3910mg,

Total Carbohydrates: 113g,

Dietary Fiber: 9g,

Sugars: 0g,

Protein: 58g

68. Brunch Burger

Preparation time: 10 minutes

Cooking time: 30 minutes

Servings: 2

Ingredients: 4 thick-cut bacon slices ½ pound ground beef Salt and pepper to taste 2–4 slices cheddar cheese 1 russet potato ½ small onion 3 eggs 2 tablespoons flour 2 tablespoons vegetable oil 2 sesame hamburger buns

Directions:

Cook the bacon in a skillet until crisp. When it is done, remove it from the skillet and set it on a plate lined with paper towel to drain. Season the ground beef with salt and pepper and form it into loose patties. Cook the burgers in the bacon grease on medium-high heat until they reach your desired doneness. Just before they are done cooking, top with a portion of the cheese. Cover, and set aside. Peel the potato and grate it into a small bowl. Grate the onion in as well. Add 1 egg, salt, pepper, and flour. Heat a clean skillet over medium-high heat and add the oil. Form the potato mixture into 2 potato pancakes and transfer them to the skillet, cooking on each side for about 3–4 minutes, or until crisp. Transfer them to a paper towel lined plate to drain. Break the remaining eggs into the skillet and cook for about 3 minutes according to your preference. Assemble your burger on a bun with bacon, egg, a potato pancake, and whatever other toppings you enjoy.

Nutrition: Calories: 1240, Total Fat: 80 g, Cholesterol: 360 mg, Sodium : 2380 mg, Total Carbohydrate: 64 g, Dietary Fiber: 5 g, Sugars: 13 g, Protein: 65 g

69. Quesadilla Burger

Preparation time: 15 minutes

Cooking time: 15 minutes

Servings: 4

Ingredients:

1 ½ pounds ground beef 8 (6-inch) flour tortillas 1 tablespoon butter

Tex-Mex seasoning for the burgers

2 teaspoons ground cumin 2 tablespoons paprika 1 teaspoon black pepper

½ teaspoon cayenne pepper, more or less depending on taste

1 teaspoon salt or to taste 1 tablespoon dried oregano

Toppings

8 slices pepper jack cheese 4 slices Applewood-smoked bacon, cooked and crumbled

½ cup shredded iceberg lettuce

Pico de Galo

1-2 Roma tomatoes, deseeded and diced thin

½-1 tablespoon thinly diced onion (red or yellow is fine) 1-2 teaspoons fresh lime juice

1-2 teaspoons fresh cilantro, chopped finely

1-2 teaspoons thinly diced jalapeños pepper

Salt and pepper to taste

Tex-Mex ranch dressing

½ cup sour cream ½ cup ranch dressing such as Hidden Valley

1 teaspoon Tex-Mex seasoning ¼ cup mild salsa

Pepper to taste

For serving (optional)

Guacamole, and sour cream

Directions

In a mixing bowl, combine the Tex-Mex seasoning ingredients and stir to ensure they are well combined. Prepare the fresh Pico de Gallo by mixing all the ingredients in a bowl. Set aside in the refrigerator until ready to use. Prepare the Tex-Mex ranch dressing by mixing all the ingredients in a bowl. Set aside in the refrigerator until ready to use. Add 2 tablespoons of the Tex-Mex seasoning to the ground beef and mix it in, being careful not to overwork the beef or your burgers will be tough. Form into 4 large ¼-inch thick burger patties and cook either on the grill or in a skillet to your preference. Heat a clean skillet over medium-low heat. Butter each of the flour tortillas on one side. Place one butter side down in the skillet. Top with 1 slice of cheese, some shredded lettuce, some Pico de Gallo, some bacon, and then top with a cooked burger. Top the burger with some of the Tex-Mex ranch dressing sauce to taste, some Pico the Gallo, bacon, and another slice of cheese. Cover with another tortilla, butter side up. Cook for about 1 minute or until the tortilla is golden. Then carefully flip the tortilla and cook until the cheese has melted. This step can be done in a sandwich press if you have one. Cut the tortillas in quarters or halves and serve with a side of the Tex-Mex ranch dressing, guacamole, and sour cream, if desired.

Nutrition: Calories: 1330, Total Fat: 93 g, Cholesterol: 240 mg, Sodium : 3000 mg, Total Carbohydrate: 50 g, Dietary Fiber: 6 g, Sugars: 7 g, Protein: 74 g

70. Honey Barbecue Riblets

Preparation time: 25 minutes

Cooking time: 2-5 hours

Servings: 4

Ingredients:

2 racks pork baby back ribs (or riblets if you can find them), about 2 ¼ pounds

Salt to taste

Pepper to taste

Garlic powder to taste

½ teaspoon liquid smoke

For the sauce

1 cup ketchup

½ cup corn syrup

½ cup honey

¼ cup apple cider vinegar

¼ cup water

2 tablespoons molasses

2 teaspoons dry mustard

2 teaspoons garlic powder

1 teaspoon chili powder

1 teaspoon onion powder

¼ teaspoon liquid smoke flavor

Directions

Preheat the oven to 275°F.

Season the ribs with salt, pepper, and garlic powder.

Place a wire rack in the bottom of a large roasting pan. Pour in about a half a cup of water and ½ teaspoon of liquid smoke.

Place the ribs on the rack, making sure they are not touching the liquid. Seal the roasting pan with either the lid or aluminum foil.

Place the pan in the oven and cook for 2–5 hours, depending on how many ribs you are cooking. Check every so often for desired tenderness. (You can speed this process up if you have an Instant Pot or other pressure cooker.)

Meanwhile, in a medium saucepan, combine all the ingredients for the sauce and bring it to a boil. Reduce the heat and let it simmer for 20 minutes.

When the ribs have reached the desired tenderness, remove them from the oven and place them on a baking sheet. Set the oven to broil. Brush the ribs with barbecue sauce and broil until the sauce starts to turn a little brown/black. Be careful not to let it burn.

Remove the ribs from the oven and serve with additional barbecue sauce.

Nutrition:

Calories: 693.4, Total Fat: 44.8 g, Cholesterol: 178.6 mg, Sodium 804.2 mg, Potassium: 500.3 mg, Total Carbohydrate: 35.5 g, Dietary Fiber: 0.2 g, Sugars: 34.1 g, Protein: 37.0 g

Chapter 6 Bread and Soup

71. Biscuits and Sausage Gravy

Preparation Time: 5 minutes

Cooking Time: 10 minutes

Servings: 2

Ingredients:

1/4-pound bulk pork sausage

2 tablespoons butter

2 to 3 tablespoons all-purpose flour

1/4 teaspoon salt

1/8 teaspoon pepper

1-1/4 to 1-1/3 cups whole milk

Warm biscuits

Directions:

In a small skillet, cook sausage over medium heat until no longer pink; drain.

Add butter and heat until melted.

Add the flour, salt, and pepper; cook and stir until blended.

Gradually add the milk, stirring constantly.

Bring to a boil; cook and stir until thickened, about 2 minutes.

Serve with biscuits.

Nutrition:

Calories: 337,

Fat: 27g,

Saturated fat: 14g

Cholesterol: 72mg,

Sodium: 718mg,

Carbohydrate: 14g, Sugar: 8g,

Fiber: 0g, Protein: 10g

72. Buttermilk Biscuits

Preparation Time: 15 minutes

Cooking Time: 15 minutes

Servings: 10

Ingredients:

2 cups all-purpose flour 2 teaspoons baking powder 1/2 teaspoon baking soda

1/2 teaspoon salt 1/4 cup shortening 3/4 cup buttermilk

Directions:

Preheat oven to 450°.

In a bowl, combine flour, baking powder, baking soda and salt; cut in shortening until the mixture resembles coarse crumbs.

Stir in buttermilk; knead dough gently.

Roll out to 1/2-in. thickness.

Cut with a 2-1/2-in. biscuit cutter and place on a lightly greased baking sheet.

Bake until golden brown, 10-15 minutes.

Freeze option: Freeze cooled biscuits in a resealable freezer container. To use, heat in a preheated 350° oven 15-20 minutes.

Nutrition:

Calories: 142, Fat: 5g, Cholesterol: 1mg, Sodium: 281mg,

Carbohydrate: 20g, Protein: 3g

73. Breadsticks

Preparation Time: 60 minutes

Cooking Time: 15 minutes

Servings: 16

Ingredients: 1½ cups warm water 2 tablespoons sugar

Breadsticks ¼ cup butter 1 teaspoon garlic powder

1 packet (1 tablespoon/¾ ounce) yeast 2 tablespoons butter, softened

2 teaspoons fine sea salt (and a bit extra to sprinkle on top)

4–5 cups bread flour (you can also use all-purpose flour, but the breadsticks will turn out denser)

Topping

Directions:

To make the breadsticks, combine the warm water, sugar, and yeast in a large bowl. Proof for 10 minutes. Mix in the salt, softened butter, and 3 cups of bread flour. Mix in the rest of the bread flour to get a soft dough. Cover the bowl with a damp towel and set aside in a warm place. Let dough rise for 1 hour. Gently knead the dough and separate into 14–16 balls. Roll each ball into a log of your desired length. Place on two cookie sheets and let rise for 15–30 minutes. To make the topping, melt the butter and mix with the garlic powder. Brush the topping mixture over the breadsticks and finish with sprinkles of sea salt. Bake at 400°F for 12–14 minutes. Brush the remaining garlic butter on top of the breadsticks.

Nutrition: Calories 190, Total Fat 4.4 g, Cholesterol 0 mg, Sodium 328 mg, Potassium 57 mg, Total Carbohydrate 31 g, Dietary fiber 1.4 g, Sugar 0.6 g, Protein 6 g

74. Chicken Gnocchi Soup

Preparation Time: 10 minutes

Cooking Time: 8 minutes

Servings: 4

Ingredients:

1 tablespoon oil 1½ pounds chicken breast, cubed ½ cup celery, chopped

½ cup onion, chopped 2 cups chicken broth 1 cup matchstick carrots

1 teaspoon thyme 3 cups half and half 1 (16-ounce) package gnocchi

2 cups fresh spinach

Directions:

Place oil, chicken, and celery in the Instant Pot. Sauté until meat is brown.

Mix in chicken broth, carrots, and thyme. Close the lid and the pressure release valve.

Set to Manual, High Pressure for 4 minutes. Once completed, quick release pressure.

Open the lid and set to sauté. Add spinach, half and half and gnocchi. Leave Instant Pot on sauté to heat the soup until it is boiling.

Let boil and keep stirring for 3 minutes or until gnocchi is cooked. Serve.

Nutrition: Calories 405, Total Fat 14g, Cholesterol 109mg,

Sodium 917mg, Potassium 798mg, Total Carbohydrates 39g, Dietary Fiber 3.3g,

Sugars 6.2g, Protein 31g

75. Zuppa Toscana

Preparation Time: 20 minutes

Cooking Time: 4 hours

Servings: 8

Ingredients: 1-pound ground hot Italian sausage 1 tablespoon garlic, minced

1 yellow onion, chopped 4 russet potatoes, diced 1-quart chicken broth

1 bunch kale ¾ cup heavy whipping cream ¼ cup parmesan, shredded

Directions:

In a large skillet, crumble the Italian sausage and cook on medium-high heat for about 5–8 minutes.

Add the onions and garlic and cook for about 2–3 minutes.

Drain the grease and move the cooked sausages and veggies to a 6-quart crock pot (or larger). Add the diced potatoes and season with salt and pepper.

Pour in enough chicken broth to cover the potatoes. Add up to 2 cups of water if there is not enough chicken broth. Stir, then cover. Set to cook on low for 5–6 hours or high for 3–4 hours. Add the kale and heavy whipping cream. Stir Replace the cover and let cook for another 30 minutes on high. Serve topped with parmesan cheese.

Nutrition: Calories 220, Total Fat 15 g, Saturated Fat 7 g, rans Fat 0 g,

Cholesterol 40 mg, Sodium   790 mg, Total Carbohydrate   15 g,

Dietary Fiber 2 g, Sugars   2 g,   Protein   7 g

76.   Pasta e Fagioli

Preparation Time: 15 minutes

Cooking Time: 35 minutes

Servings: 6

Ingredients:

2 tablespoons olive oil (divided)

1-pound lean ground beef 1½ cups yellow onion, chopped

1 cup (about 2 medium) carrots, diced 1 cup (about 3 stalks) celery, diced

3 cloves (1 tablespoon) garlic, minced

3 cups tomato sauce 2 (14½-ounce) cans low-sodium chicken broth

½ cup water, then more as desired

1 (15-ounce) can diced tomatoes 2 teaspoons sugar

1½ teaspoons dried basil 1 teaspoon dried oregano

¾ teaspoon dried thyme ½ teaspoon dried marjoram

Salt and freshly ground black pepper

1 cup dry ditalini pasta

1 (15-ounce) can dark red kidney beans, drained and rinsed

1 (15-ounce) can great northern beans, drained and rinsed

Finely shredded Romano or parmesan cheese, for serving

3 tablespoons fresh parsley, minced

Directions:

In a large pot, cook ground beef or sausage in 1 tablespoon of olive oil on medium-high heat. Stir and leave to cook until brown.

Drain grease and remove the meat from the pot. Heat the other tablespoon of olive oil to cook the onions, carrots, and celery. Sauté on medium-high heat for about 6 minutes.

Add garlic and sauté for 1 minute. Mix in chicken broth, tomato sauce, cooked meat, water, canned tomatoes, sugar, basil, oregano, thyme, and marjoram. Add salt and pepper to taste.

Bring soup to a boil, then lower to medium-low heat, cover and simmer for 15–20 minutes, stirring occasionally.

Follow directions on ditalini pasta package to cook to al dente. Add the cooked pasta to the soup along with the kidney and great northern beans. Add more broth or water if needed. Cook for 1 minute longer. Mix in parsley, then serve with grated cheese, if desired.

Nutrition: Calories 150,

Total Fat   5 g,

Saturated Fat   2 g, Trans Fat   0 g,

Cholesterol   15 mg, Sodium   710 mg   ,

Total Carbohydrate 16 g, Dietary Fiber   3 g,

Sugars   4 g,   Protein   8 g

77. Lima Beans

Preparation Time: 10 minutes

Cooking Time: 30 minutes

Servings: 4 to 6

Ingredients: 1 cup water 1 chicken bouillon cube 2 slices bacon, chopped

1 clove garlic, peeled and lightly mashed ½ teaspoon red pepper flakes

½ teaspoon onion powder 1 teaspoon sugar ½ teaspoon black pepper

1 (1-pound) bag frozen lima beans

Directions:

Add the water and bouillon cube to a large pot and bring to a boil.

Stir in the remaining ingredients. Cover and turn the heat down so that the beans are simmering slightly.

Allow to simmer for 30 minutes, stirring occasionally. (Add more water if necessary.)

Remove the garlic and then, season with salt and pepper to taste.

Nutrition:

Calories: 290, Total Fat: 15g, Saturated Fat: 3g, Cholesterol: 30mg,

Sodium   : 320 mg,   Total Carbohydrate: 29 g,

Dietary Fiber: 7 g,   Sugars: 0g,   Protein:10 g

78. Toasted Ravioli

Preparation Time: 10 minutes

Cooking Time: 10 minutes

Servings: 4 to 6

Ingredients: 1 (1-pound) package meat ravioli, thawed 2 eggs ¼ cup water

1 teaspoon garlic salt 1 cup flour 1 cup breadcrumbs ½ teaspoon oregano

1 teaspoon basil

Grated parmesan (for garnish)

Directions:

Add the eggs and water to a small bowl. Beat together.

To another bowl, add the oregano, basil, garlic salt, and breadcrumbs. Combine together.

To a third bowl, add the flour. Heat oil to 350°F.

Dip the ravioli in the flour, then the eggs, then the breadcrumbs. Repeat for each and set aside.

Place in oil and fry until golden brown. Place on a cooling rack or paper towel to drain some of the oil. If desired, sprinkle with parmesan. Serve with marinara sauce.

Nutrition:

Calories: 580, Total Fat: 28 g, Cholesterol: 35 mg, Sodium : 830 mg,

Total Carbohydrate: 61 g, Dietary Fiber: 5 g, Sugar: 7 g,   Protein: 22 g

79. Chicken Potpie

Preparation Time: 10 minutes

Cooking Time: 20 minutes

Servings: 6

Ingredients: 2 tablespoons canola oil 1 medium onion, chopped

1/2 cup all-purpose flour 1 teaspoon poultry seasoning

1 can (14-1/2 ounces) chicken broth 3/4 cup 2% milk 3 cups cubed cooked chicken

2 cups frozen mixed vegetables (about 10 ounces), thawed

1 sheet refrigerated pie crust

Directions:

Preheat oven to 450°. In a large saucepan, heat oil over medium-high heat. Add onion; cook and stir until tender. Stir in flour and poultry seasoning until blended; gradually whisk in broth and milk. Bring to a boil, stirring constantly; cook and stir 2-3 minutes or until thickened. Stir in chicken and vegetables.Transfer to a greased 9-in. deep-dish pie plate; place crust over filling. Trim, seal, and flute edges. Cut slits in crust.

Bake 15-20 minutes or until crust is golden brown and filling is bubbly.

Nutrition:

Calories: 439, Fat: 20g Cholesterol: 73mg, Sodium: 526mg,

Carbohydrate: 37g, Protein: 26g

80. Roast Beef Sandwiches with Mashed Potatoes

Preparation Time: 7 minutes

Cooking Time: 3 minutes

Servings: 4

Ingredients:

1-pound sliced deli roast beef

2 cans (10-1/4 ounces each) beef gravy

1 can (4 ounces) mushroom stems and pieces, drained

1 package (3-3/4 ounces) creamy butter instant mashed potatoes

4 slices Italian bread (1/2 inch thick)

Directions:

In a 2-qt. microwave-safe bowl, combine the beef, gravy, and mushrooms. Cover and microwave on high for 2-3 minutes or until heated through.

Meanwhile, prepare potatoes according to package directions. Divide bread among four plates. Spoon beef mixture over bread. Serve with potatoes.

Nutrition:

Calories: 347, Fat: 7g, Cholesterol: 75mg, Sodium: 2051mg, Carbohydrate: 38g, Protein: 30g

81. Corn Chowder

Preparation Time: 10 minutes

Cooking Time: 40 minutes

Servings: 4

Ingredients: 4 garlic cloves, minced   ½ cup red bell pepper   1 ½ cups heavy cream

½ cup green bell pepper, diced   4 tablespoons unsalted butter

1 jalapeño pepper, medium, seeded & chopped finely   ¼ cup all-purpose flour

5 cups vegetable stock, low sodium   1 white onion, medium, chopped

4 cups sweet corn kernels, fresh   ½ teaspoon cracked black pepper

1 russet potato, diced   2 plum tomatoes, diced   ¼ teaspoon ground cayenne pepper

3 tablespoons fresh cilantro, chopped   1 tablespoon white wine vinegar

¾ teaspoon smoked paprika   1 tablespoon lime juice, freshly squeezed

2 teaspoons salt

Directions: Over medium heat in a large, heavy-bottomed pot; heat the butter until melted. Add green bell pepper together with jalapeño, onion, garlic, and red bell pepper to the pot with melted butter, sauté for a couple of minutes. Add in the all-purpose flour; give everything a good stir until you get thick paste like consistency. Stir in the corn kernels, heavy cream, vegetable stock, Russet potato, smoked paprika, cayenne pepper, black pepper, and salt. Bring everything together to a gentle simmer; cover & cook until the mixture has thickened, and potatoes have softened, for 20 minutes. Stir in the white wine vinegar, lime juice, tomatoes & cilantro; let simmer for 5 more minutes. Serve immediately & enjoy.

Nutrition:

Calories 238, Total Fat 15 g, Cholesterol 26 mg, Sodium 718 mg,

Total Carbohydrate 18 g, Dietary fiber 2.2 g, Protein 7 g

82. Squash Soup

Preparation Time: 20 minutes

Cooking Time: 45 minutes

Servings: 10

Ingredients: 2 pounds butternut squash; peeled & cut into 1" cubes

½ teaspoon cinnamon 1 cup white onion, chopped 15 ounces pumpkin

2 cups vegetable stock 1 tablespoon honey 2 teaspoons curry powder or to taste

1 cup apple juice 2 tablespoon vegetable oil, divided 1 tablespoon pumpkin seeds

½ cup heavy cream

Directions:

Preheat your oven to 350 F in advance. Drizzle 1 tablespoon of vegetable oil on top of the butternut squash; stir until coated well. Bake in the preheated oven until the butternut squash is fork tender, for 30 minutes. Do not let the squash brown. Now, heat 1 tablespoon of the vegetable oil over moderate heat in a large stock pot & sauté the onions for a couple of minutes, until translucent. As you sauté the onions; sprinkle a small amount of salt on top of them. When done; immediately add in the butternut squash, pumpkin, curry powder, vegetable stock, apple juice, cinnamon, & honey. Heat through. Make the soup smooth using an immersion blender. Add cream to the soup; give everything a good stir. Toast the pumpkin seeds over moderate heat in a small skillet. Heat through until fragrant, for a few minutes. Immediately remove from heat. Serve and enjoy.

Nutrition: Calories 110, Total Fat 2.5g, Cholesterol 5mg, Sodium 750mg,

Carbohydrates 22g, Fiber 2g, Glucose 10g, Protein 2g

83. Cuban Sandwich

Preparation time: 20 minutes

Cooking time: 5 minutes

Servings: 4

Ingredients: ½ teaspoon olive oil 2 garlic cloves, minced

½ cup reduced-fat mayonnaise 8 slices artisan bread

8 thick slices deli smoked turkey 4 slices deli ham 8 slices Swiss cheese

12 dill pickle slices 1 cup fresh baby spinach

Directions:

Heat the olive oil in a small skillet. Add the garlic and cook until the garlic is fragrant. Remove it from the heat and let it cool, then stir it into the mayonnaise.

Spread some garlic mayo over each slice of bread, and assemble the sandwiches using turkey, ham, cheese, pickles, and spinach.

Cook the sandwiches in a Panini maker or grill them in skillet until the cheese melts and the bread has browned up.

Serve.

Nutrition:

Calories: 475, Total Fat: 14.3g, Cholesterol: 41mg, Sodium: 1770mg,

Carbohydrates: 60.4g Carbohydrates 57.3g, Fiber: 3.1g, Glucose: 7.6g, Protein 26.3g

84. Chicken Noodle Soup

Preparation Time: 5 minutes

Cooking Time: 4 hours & 15 minutes

Servings: 6

Ingredients 2 boneless, skinless chicken breasts 1 cup egg noodles

2 cups water or as required onion, small, diced 2 cans chicken broth

1 teaspoon thyme 2 cups celery, diced 1 bay leaf 2 cups carrots, diced

1 teaspoon minced garlic or garlic salt Pepper and salt to taste

Directions:

Place the entire ingredients (except the egg noodles) in the bottom of your crock pot; give everything a good stir until evenly combined.

Cover & cook for 3 to 4 hours on high-heat or 6 to 8 hours on low-heat.

Just 30 minutes before you serve this soup, remove the chicken pieces & shred.

Place them to the pot again. Turn on the high of your crock pot & add in the egg noodles; let cook for half an hour.

Serve immediately and enjoy.

Nutrition:

Calories: 124, Total Fat: 4.7g, Cholesterol: 25mg, Sodium: 1731mg,

Potassium: 109mg, Carbohydrates: 15g

Conclusion

Creativity often happens when you cook at home, and you can attach a range of plant foods to a variety of colors. You are not only acquiring kilograms, antioxidants, minerals, and phytonutrients, but also introducing nice textures and colors to your meals. You would be shocked by how much food in a single dish is collected.

Portion control from home can be regulated. When food is cooked for us, we tend to eat all or most of it. Try to use little dishes at home, but ensure that all good things like vegetables, fruits, whole grains, and legumes are filled. You are certainly going to be satisfied and happy.

The biggest advantage of using copycat restaurant recipes is that not only can you save money, but, if needed, you can customize the recipes. For example, if you want to reduce the salt or butter in one of the plates, you can. Now you have saved money, and at the same time provided a nutritious meal for your family.

Trying to guess what the ingredients are to your favorite restaurant meal is eliminated when you use copycat recipes. You simply follow the recipe, and slowly recreate your favorite meal.

It is not really that difficult to learn how to cooktop secret restaurant recipes. Some think you need a degree in culinary arts or cooking education so you can cook those secret recipes. However, anyone can collect the ingredients themselves and cook a fancy meal that tastes like the real thing.

But do top secret restaurant recipes really taste the way the chef served them? Perhaps. You can easily cook your favorite recipes with a little practice and patience. You would just want to cook the basic formula and start adding what you think would make the flavor of the recipe better after a while. You may start to figure out that some recipes might need a little more herbs or peppers to make the dish better than the original! But if you've ever badly prepared food of this kind on your own, there is hope! With just a few simple tricks and tips, you can also cook quality cuisine in your own kitchen. These tricks may not seem so strong on their own but can transform how you prepare and produce food when they are all used together. These tips help you cook at home like a pro from expired spices and how you use salt to literally arrange it before you start cooking.

When preparing desserts at home, you can tweak the recipes as you wish. As you sample the recipes, you will get to know the usual ingredients and techniques in making popular sweet treats. This could inspire you to create your very own recipes. You can substitute ingredients as your taste, health, or pocket dictates. You can come up, perhaps, not with a dessert that is the perfect clone of a restaurant's recipe, but with one that is exactly the way you want it to be. Most of all, the recipes here are meant for you to experience the fulfillment of seeing the smiles on the people with whom you share your creations. Keep trying and having fun with the recipes and you will soon be reaping your sweet rewards!

If prepared food arrives from outside the home you typically have limited knowledge about salt, sugar, and processed oils. For fact, we also apply more to our meal when it is served to the table. You will say how much salt, sugar and oil is being used as you prepare meals at home.

Copycat recipes practically give you the ability to make great restaurant food tasting in your own home and get it right first time and easily.

CPSIA information can be obtained
at www.ICGtesting.com
Printed in the USA
BVHW011436080321
601999BV00002B/92

9 781801 645065